LAW OF GLOBAL COMMERCE

A TOUR

David M. Neipert

JOB SKILLS
NETEFFECT SERIES

Prentice Hall

Upper Saddle River, NJ 07458

Library of Congress Cataloging-in-Publication Data

Neipert, David.
   Law of global commerce: a tour / David M. Neipert.
      p. cm.
   Includes index.
   ISBN 0-13-040873-5
   1. Business law. 2. Commercial law. 3. Foreign trade regulation. I. Title.

K1005.N45 2002
346.07—dc21

2001036178

Executive Editor: Elizabeth Sugg
Publisher: Steve Helba
Editorial Assistant: Anita Rhodes
Managing Editor: Mary Carnis
Production Editor: Brian Hyland
Director of Production and Manufacturing: Bruce Johnson
Manufacturing Buyer: Cathleen Petersen
Design Director: Cheryl Asherman
Senior Design Coordinator: Miguel Ortiz
Net Effect Series Design: Rob Richman/LaFortezza Design Group
Composition: BookMasters, Inc.
Full-Service Production Management: BookMasters, Inc.
Printer/Binder: RR Donnelly–Harrisonburg

Pearson Education LTD.
Pearson Education Australia PTY, Limited
Pearson Education Singapore, Pte. Ltd
Pearson Education North Asia Ltd
Pearson Education Canada, Ltd.
Pearson Educación de Mexico, S.A. de C.V.
Pearson Education—Japan
Pearson Education Malaysia, Pte. Ltd
Pearson Education, Upper Saddle River, New Jersey

10 9 8 7 6 5 4 3 2 1
ISBN 0-13-040873-5

Contents

Preface

Preparing for a career in international business is a daunting task. A businessperson stepping off an airplane in a foreign land often encounters profound changes in business technique. Conversations take place in a different language; personalities and negotiating postures are dramatically different; unfamiliar tax systems come into play; and curious religious practices may bias the process. Not least of all, the legal environment may be strange and threatening. If the problems of international business are daunting, however, the opportunities are magnificent. Languages can be learned, interpersonal skills polished, experts hired to help, the risks assessed, and the deal made. Hopefully, the result will be profits and personal satisfaction.

The books available concerning international legal topics are generally written on narrow topics for lawyers and law students. They contain much information of little value to business, such as the methods used to resolve disputes between governments. Often they do not explain the principles of the national legal systems that will govern the part of any transaction that falls in the foreign courts. Many international business law books contain so much law terminology, they may be more indecipherable than the language spoken in the foreign country! And many contain more footnotes and bibliography than text. Most existing international law books are devoid of cultural and historical perspective, which makes it difficult for the student to truly understand how the law is likely to be applied.

International business is important at the University of Texas Pan American and the University of Tartu where this book was written and first used. I like to use just the right teaching materials for my students. This book is a "just right" combination of background material and law.

This book contains information to address the legal problems that international business activities most frequently encounter. It is written for business students and business practitioners, not lawyers, though many lawyers have told me they enjoyed reading it. It is written like a newspaper, completely without "legalese" and "academese," and it should be easy to understand, even for those who have English as a second language. After reading this book, the reader will have a basic understanding of the following concepts:

1. How business activities are viewed by each of the major legal systems in use around the world today.

2. The historical and cultural perspective of business law around the world that influences the thought process of the foreign lawyer or judge.

3. The international law that regulates international trade and transport.

4. The major trading agreements in force and how they affect trade and investment within and without their boundaries.

5. The legal status of persons working in foreign countries.

6. How international business disputes are resolved.

7. How different nations regulate advertising and marketing activities.

8. When to get expert help with international legal problems.

9. The structure of international sales and investments and the enforcement of intellectual property rights.

This book, therefore, touches several academic disciplines, among them business, comparative and international law, and a smattering of history and culture. I have tired to write it in a way that is interesting to read. If I have succeeded in that, the credit belongs to three extraordinary high school teachers, named Browning, Darnell, and Inman who patiently taught me how to write. Because they were, perhaps, better at teaching than I was as their student, I thank Prentice Hall's equally extraordinary copy editors who help me look good when they have finished improving this book as they did with my former volume, A *Tour of International Trade.*

I am also grateful for the support I have received from the Accounting and Business Law Department at the University of Texas Pan American where I am based. I also appreciate the support received from the Eurofaculty of the University of Tartu Law School in Estonia. I finished the book there while I was lecturing as a visiting Fulbright Scholar.

This book, in its nearly final form, was first used there in Estonia with students for whom English was a foreign language. The comments, suggestions, and perspectives of my Estonian students were helpful in making my final revisions and in achieving my goal of writing a law book that anyone who had mastered the language reasonably well could understand. These students were my true reviewers, and their success in mastering the content is my best reward for this effort. I will always remember my days and students in Tartu with fondness and gratitude.

I am proud of this book. I know that it will help prepare the student for the real world of international business.

Comments from Our Readers

"...I particularly enjoyed the first section, 'Legal Systems of the World'. The historical background provided in these chapters I had not encountered in other books."

—Dr. Robert Girling, Sonoma State University

"...I do like his breadth of subject coverage."

—Dr. Peter Banfe, Ohio Northern University

"Excellent writing—great narration—exhaustive content."

—Mustafa Savliwala, Davenport College

Section I

Legal Systems of the World

The hundreds of sovereign nations in the world each have their own courts and laws. Today, even a medium-sized company may do business in dozens of separate nations. Such a company will, therefore, be charged with the task of compliance with local law in each jurisdiction. Also, management must make decisions about whether to enter a new country where it has not conducted business in the past. The legal scheme of that country will enter into the equation of that decision, particularly if the industry is a heavily regulated one. How does management keep up with the basics of so many national legal arrangements?

Although law is fundamentally a national institution, various national legal systems exhibit patterns and parallels, which are the subject of this section. Most nations in the world today use one of only a few legal systems as the basis of their laws. Former colonies may use a mixture of them. One can understand the basics of the legal system of any given country if one understands the basics of the legal system upon which the laws of that country are based. In this section we shall explore the world's major legal systems from a historical, cultural, and legal perspective.

Business decisions require judgments to be made on a variety of questions and the legal environment figures into many of these decisions. Here are some examples:

1. Can we insure our factory against fire in country W?

2. Is country X likely to enforce a certain type of sales contract?

3. Would a male or female witness be more credible to the courts in country Y?

4. Is country Z a place likely to promptly evict a deadbeat tenant?

All of these questions have significant legal aspects. The answers vary widely from place to place. Even though no book of this type can give specific answers to all such questions, a basic understanding of the legal systems in use in the world today will be of value in making the business decision. It will also help the business professional recognize when hazardous legal territory is being approached and local expertise is needed.

Most of the world's people live under the <u>auspices</u> of one of the major legal systems presented in the following pages. Often one system dominates, but the influence of others is also evident. Before we look specifically at these systems, let's take a look at the concept of law itself within the context of basic human nature as the same everywhere, even if local conditions are not.

After we explore the world's legal systems we shall examine other aspects of law and international law of importance to world business.

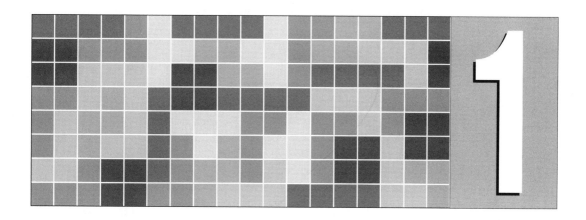

Our Tour Begins:
The Dawn of Law

Consider for a moment a hypothetical primitive tribe. The tribal chief must deal with a plethora of problems.

1. The men are fighting with each other over the women.

2. Nobody wants to take much time or trouble to make something useful because it would be stolen the moment the maker goes to sleep.

3. The most trivial argument may result in a homicide.

4. It is difficult to ascertain the truth about anything because all members will tell lies in order to secure an advantage.

5. The older members, who have accumulated the wisdom and expertise of the years, are scorned because of their physical weakness.

6. Countless arguments erupt over questions such as which god should be worshiped and other religious matters.

Hostile tribes that would like to possess the lands occupied by this tribe surround the tribe. A battle looms and victory is unlikely because the tribe is weakened considerably by the internal conflicts and other problems already mentioned. If this tribe is to persevere, some changes are essential.

The chief could call a meeting and announce some new rules. Here are some possibilities:

1. Each man takes one woman as his mate for life and that relationship must be respected by the other men and women.

2. Thievery is not permitted.

3. Murder is also prohibited.

4. Old people are to be respected and assisted.

5. The chief's god is everybody's god.

Breaking one of these rules results in some predetermined punishment. This type of rule comprises the basic social compact by which civilizations can be formed. The tribe that does not adopt such rules will be torn by inner conflict and will not survive.

Those schooled in Judeo-Christian theology will recognize such rules as some of the Ten Commandments, but nearly every advanced tribe or civilization in the world has similar restrictions on the behavior of its members.

The basic conventions that allow people to interact peacefully and prosper are nearly universal because basic human nature is the same everywhere. Generally, the rules one follows at home will apply abroad. A business trip abroad to a country you are not familiar with is not the place to go on a drinking binge, experiment with drugs, and otherwise do things you would not do if your friends and family were watching.

But rules differ, partly because conditions around the planet differ. Some societies are located on islands, some are on huge continents. Some people live in densely populated areas, others in sparsely populated regions. Restrictions appropriate in mountains may not make sense in deserts. Some societies separate law and religion, and others make these two factors virtually inseparable. So although many fundamentals are uniform, the law has developed differently to adjust to local conditions.

In the next chapters we shall look at legal systems around the world in the context of their underlying societies and gain some insight into how business can be conducted within the framework of that legal system.

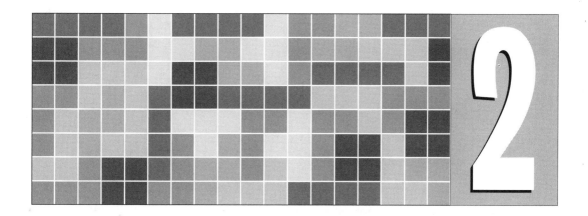

A Tour of Romano-Germanic Law

Most European nations use a legal system called Romano-Germanic or Civil Law. It is distinguished by the fact that it is not based directly on religion, is well organized, and is written into comprehensive codes. Each code contains the requirements for one particular area of regulation. Examples include a criminal code, a business code, a marriage code, and a code governing family relationships.

Each code is a comprehensive list of the legal principles that should govern a judge's decisions in that area of law. Knowing the history of the development of such codes aids in understanding their application and is also interesting reading.

Many scholars begin their discussion of the law of Europe with praise for Emperor Justinian from whose name the words justice, jurisprudence, jury, judicial, judge, and so on are derived. This book will not begin with him. He did not originate the idea of a legal code and is not worthy of the honor in any case. An explanation follows later in the chapter.

Our discussion begins instead in what is present-day Iraq, but about 3,750 years ago. At that time, and in most subsequent world history, any law in force in the world was simply decreed by a person capable of inflicting

判沢/rule

great violence if he or she were disobeyed. Law was originally a collection of the whims of powerful tribal chieftains. Most law was intended to perpetuate the domination and power of the authority that decreed it. Little consideration was given to the effect of the law on the lives of the private citizens, and no regard shown for what we call "human rights" today.

An example of the brutality of early law that was actually enacted much later in history would be the laws promulgated by a Greek named Draco in 621 B.C. His laws were so oppressive, particularly with his liberal use of the death penalty for even minor offenses, that the word *draconian* derives from his name.

This sort of law, however, would pass by the wayside as people became more civilized, and nearly 40 centuries ago change was already in the works. The world's first great city was forming in the area where Baghdad stands today. A great city needs some semblance of regulation to preserve order and enforce the social compact between the members. This first real metropolis, called Babylon, was a conglomeration of several cities in the area.

In the earliest history of Babylon the neighboring cities fought each other for control of the area. The city whose military was in charge at the moment imposed tributes against the others without otherwise greatly affecting life there. Each city retained its separate tribal rules and customs. The population of the various cities was multiracial in character. Commerce between the cities was commonplace. It would take a versatile ruler to unite this area. Eventually, he showed up.

Babylon was united by force of arms into a single nation under a remarkable ruler named Hammurabi. Change in the administration of justice was swift. Hammurabi wanted his law to be uniform throughout Babylon and he wanted it to be a means of achieving social justice. In setting out the law, he declared his purpose: "[T]o bring about the rule of righteousness in the land, to destroy the wicked and the evil-doers; so that the strong should not harm the weak; . . . and enlighten the land, to further the well-being of mankind."

Hammurabi also wanted his law to be orderly and complete, in contrast to the piecemeal decrees that had proceeded him. In writing his legal code, he generally deleted meaningless tribal customs from the law. Then he assembled, in an orderly fashion, the forerunner of a modern legal code. It protected families, children, and marriages and provided for adoption of orphans. It set forth the grounds for divorce and subsequent property settlement. The code punished criminals and defined standards for evidence. It gave certain rights to women and slaves. It had provisions for inheritance after the death of the owner. It had provisions for payment of damages for medical malpractice. It regulated lending activities, real estate sales and rentals, water rights, and farming activities. Minimum wages were set for free workers. An agency law was established to regulate those merchants whose caravans were engaged in marketing goods for others. Finally, a right to an appeal of a legal decision to a higher court was granted.

These laws, which consist of 282 separate statutes, were carved onto stones and displayed so that they were accessible to the populace. The result was a uniform legal system for the entire empire. One such stone from the time of Hammurabi survives to this day and is now in the Louvre Museum in Paris.

In the years that followed Hammurabi, more Dracos appeared than Hammurabis, but the concept that law should serve the ends of humanity and justice survived the ages and is incorporated into modern western legal systems.

In the following ages, a number of rudimentary legal codes appeared. By the time the Roman Empire ruled the Western world, a code ruled the empire. The Roman code was not authored by emperor Justinian. Rather, it evolved over the centuries while the capital of the empire was in Rome. Justinian did reorganize and edit the code and his story is worth telling, if only to dispel some myths.

The story begins with Emperor Constantine about 300 years after the death of Christ. He inherited an empire in shambles. Rome was no longer militarily defensible, and an assortment of Huns, Goths, Visigoth, and others with malevolent intentions periodically swarmed over the northern borders of the empire. Religious strife also disturbed the empire, and not all the religions were obliging to the authority of the Roman government.

Many think the empire "fell" about this time, but that is not the case. Adjustments were made to accommodate the harsh realities, and the empire continued. Emperor Constantine made Christianity the official religion. One explanation is that he was divinely inspired, but others suspect that Christianity's tolerance and policy of noninterference with secular government may have factored into the emperor's choice. Constantine also moved the capital east to a Greek colony called Byzantium in what is modern day Turkey.

Byzantium was quite defensible with one side protected by the sea and the others with triple walls. Constantine changed the name of the city to Constantinople in honor of himself. The city was, in its time, a modern marvel with such amenities as police protection, a fire brigade, planned straight wide streets, and a welfare system for the poor. Roman rule and Christianity continued there until the Ottoman Turks captured the place a thousand years later and changed the name again to Istanbul. This eastern part of the Roman Empire was called the Byzantine Empire even though it was Roman in all respects but name. The citizens still called themselves Romans but the empire was no longer in Rome. Perhaps the name change confused many into thinking that the fall of the Roman Empire happened about A.D. 300. Roman Constantinople actually fell to the Turks in A.D. 1453.

The story of Justinian begins and continues in Constantinople's equivalent of the Roman Coliseum, a stadium called the Hippodrome. It was there that his wife to be, Theodora began her career as what we might today describe as an "exotic dancer," performing for the stadium's multitudes without the luxury of any sort of costume. But Theodora had better things in mind for her future. It could be said that her ambition was as naked as her body.

Justinian succeeded to the throne in 527 and began a series of military campaigns to recapture lands that had been lost to the empire. He was at least temporarily successful, but the cost of his campaigns exhausted the treasury and resulted in the need to levy heavy new taxes upon the citizenry. More on all this in paragraphs to come, but first we shall examine Justinian's effect on the legal system.

In the previous days of a more democratic Rome, law had come from the Senate. By the time of Justinian, Rome had long since reverted to a monarchy, with changes to the law decreed by the Emperor. Emperors had published legal codes long before Justinian. A notable example was that of Theodosius. But Justinian decided to perpetuate his glory and authority by putting his name on a new comprehensive legal code for the empire. This code was not an original; it merely expanded upon existing codes. And Justinian did not undertake the preparation of the code personally, he appointed 10 experts to do the work for him. An original code was prepared but it was soon revised with additional legislation. The end result was a collection of about 4,600 laws organized into 10 volumes, with a few supplements later published on church law, public affairs, and a family code. The codes were written in Latin while the supplements, called *Novels*, were written in Greek, which was the common language of the area.

Justinian is given great historical credit for his new code. Although the code is basically a rewriting of older laws, the Christian conversion of the empire played a role in the philosophy of the new law. Consequently Justinian's code attempted to make the law more humane than it had been in the past. The law made a greater attempt than previous ones to protect the poor and weak from the rich and powerful. Laws protected slaves, debtors, and wives from cruelty. For these changes, which appear to make the law more compassionate, Justinian has been granted an honored place in legal history. His name has been glorified in modern legal terminology (judge, judicial, justice, judgment, etc.).

Does Justinian deserve such a great honor? No he doesn't; not at all, at least not in my opinion. Because this book is a law book more than a history book, I shall quickly finish the story of Justinian and Theodora. But I shall finish it, if only in order to advance my premise.

When Justinian was about 40 years old, and not yet emperor, he met the then 20-year-old Theodora and became infatuated with her. Justinian wished to marry her but Roman law forbade an heir to the throne from marriage to a woman who could be classified as a prostitute. Justinian convinced his father to repeal the law. He married Theodora in 525. In 527 Justinian's father stepped down and gave Justinian the throne with

Theodora sitting as empress. Together they governed the Eastern Roman Empire. It was not a happy reign.

The high taxes that were necessitated by Justinian's wars resulted in growing discontent among the populace. In 532 a huge crowd gathered in the Hippodrome demanding the appointment of a new emperor and relief from the burdensome taxes. Justinian and Theodora responded by turning a mercenary army of Germanic barbarians loose on their own citizenry. They achieved their desired result. It was the end of dissent on the level of taxation. The only downside was the need to remove 30,000 dead bodies of Roman citizens from the Hippodrome. In my estimation, this event squelched any thought of Justinian occupying an esteemed place in the history of jurisprudence. A great leader and jurist does not massacre his own citizens. In the world of law, an appropriate role for Justinian to play would be as defendant in a human rights trial. The honors for the conception of a humane legal framework should go to Hammurabi.

When the Roman Empire went east, West Europe fell into the Dark Ages. Feudal government ruled by force of arms and medieval society had neither the will nor the intellect to follow an orderly and scholarly approach to its laws. In each place, the king could do no wrong and only the church tempered the king's otherwise nearly absolute power. What trials were held often were characterized by nonrational proof such as trial by fire or combat where God was thought to have influenced the outcome in favor of justice. Kings did not concern themselves too much with judicial matters. The idea of promoting justice on Earth was widely thought to be the responsibility of the church rather than the government.

After a dark age comes a renaissance. The revival of intellect that came to Europe in the twelfth century included a revival of the concept of the rule of law. The desire was not only to return to a society ruled by law but also to improve the law's philosophical basis so that it would be based on justice and reason. The idea that secular law should be something separate from religion was accepted. The concept of trials influenced by supernatural intervention was abandoned and clerics were forbidden to take part in such trials after the thirteenth century. Even so, no modern law arose to take the place of the feudal system. Instead, scholars looked back to the Romans for a number of reasons. Roman law had been highly developed. It had been written down and had survived the Dark Ages, partly because of its continuous use in the Byzantine Empire. It was also largely written in Latin, which the Christian church had spread all around Europe. So Roman law was therefore universally understood.

Roman law became the basis for all teaching of law in Europe's new universities, and the universities took the lead in promoting the idea of the rule of law throughout the Renaissance. Roman law was the beginning point for the development of modern legal systems on continental Europe. In fact, few European universities even offered courses about local laws until the eighteenth century.

The old Roman codes were the starting point in many universities, but Roman law was not considered perfect or even well adapted to European society of the time. The process of perfecting it and updating it to local conditions resulted in large-scale modifications of the original Roman codes in many countries, particularly in Germany, and in France after the revolution.

Over the years subsequent to the Renaissance, Roman law drifted away from its original Roman roots to be a system founded on reason. Roman law was the beginning point of a search for an approach to law that would lead to just results. One fruit of this search is the concept of natural law that was widely studied in the seventeenth and eighteenth centuries. The concept of natural law was the first expression of the idea that humans had individual rights merely because they were humans and existed on the earth. The concept of a natural law had a profound effect on government because the idea of government not merely enforcing law, but itself being subject to a natural law. It limited government's powers to unjustly interfere with the lives of the citizenry and provided the basis for thought that led to the American democracy.

In practice Roman law was not complete or relevant enough to constitute the entire body of law applied by courts. Church law or canon law had been used to resolve disputes in many areas, and the application of church law continued after the church itself quit the business of administering justice. Even where church law was not directly applied, the moral influence of the church was felt in courtrooms. Local customs also figured into the daily application of the law. Law as was actually practiced in Europe had become a mixture, and by the eighteenth century was ripe for the creation of a new code.

Early in the nineteenth century the great nations of Europe, with the exception of the United Kingdom, began to codify their entire national laws. Several important ones served as models for others. France's civil code came out in 1804 followed by Germany's in 1896 and Switzerland's in 1907. These codes and the legal systems similar to them are called the *Romano-Germanic* family of laws.

Romano-Germanic law and influence spread far beyond its original birthplace in Europe due to the colonization of many parts of the world by European powers. In particular the Spanish, together with the Portuguese, French, and Dutch, established the Romano-Germanic system in the Americas where much of the <u>indigenous</u> population, without a well-developed system of law of their own, readily accepted it. Considerable differences distinguish Romano-Germanic law as practiced in the Americas today from that practiced in Europe. This change is due, no doubt, to vast differences between the two societies, but the roots of law in the Americas, outside Britain's former colonies, are clearly Romano-Germanic.

The considerable influence of Romano-Germanic law can also be seen in Africa and Madagascar, even though tribal customs have been part of, and have been recently reintroduced to, the legal system there as well. Particularly since independence, several African countries have rediscovered tribal roots. One notable exception is the Arabian Peninsula, which, although colonized by Europe, never accepted western law and largely reverted to Islamic law after gaining independence. Turkey, by contrast, has considered the adoption of Romano-Germanic law a key to modernizing its county and is shifting from its previous use of Islamic law. Many countries in North Africa, having long had relations with both Europe and the rest of Arabia, have a legal system that is a mixture of Islamic law and Romano-Germanic. Islamic law dominates traditional life defining the law of marriage, divorce, inheritance, suppression, or crime while leaving commercial and taxation matters to Romano-Germanic law.

In Asia, both China and Japan have adopted some aspects of Romano-Germanic law.

Romano-Germanic law is divided into private and public aspects. Private law has to do with disputes between private parties, and public law is concerned with the rules for operation of the government and protection of citizens from government abuses. Because the government administers public law, it is supposed to be watching the government's effectiveness. That effectiveness, however, especially in places where administration is corrupt or inept, is questionable. Private Romano-Germanic law enjoys a better reputation.

The philosophy of Romano-Germanic law is easy to grasp. The goal is to have the entire body of law on a subject condensed into a general code. The code does not try to answer directly every question that may arise in that particular area of law. Rather, the code is supposed to be a set of basic rules from which the proper resolution of a specific legal problem can be deduced. If the rule is too general, it is not of any help to someone wishing to read the law in order to find a way to avoid a conflict with it. On the other hand, it must be general enough to apply to a broad situation rather than some particular aspect of it. A more general rule also gives more discretion to the judge and a constant debate exists on just how specific code rules should be. The code should set out the general framework of the law and give the court a set of standards for its decision. If the code is too detailed it will encourage parties to find loopholes and therefore a certain amount of generality is thought to give the judge more latitude to achieve a just result.

The French have taken the path of making the law more of a general framework and giving the judge more latitude to make the final rule. The Germans have detailed codes resulting in a law that is less flexible, but more predictable, and decreases the ability of the judge to influence the outcome.

An advantage of using code law is that it has less law to sift through than does the English system of precedent and case law. In place of thousands of cases under the English system lies but one general code under the Romano-Germanic system.

 Having a more compact body of law does exact a price, however, and that price is lack of <u>precision.</u> In English law one can usually find a case that arises from nearly the specific situation presently in controversy. Everyone knows that the court is likely to make the same decision in the present case as it made in the past. The system is certain and predictable.

Under Romano-Germanic law, two judges may consider the same facts and general principles of law and formulate two separate solutions. In addition, neither one will have any effect on a future judge's consideration of the same type of case. The system is much less certain and predictable. Situations that prompt repeated conflict between courts eventually result in a new provision in the code resolving the conflict.

Today Romano-Germanic law usually comes from democratically elected legislative bodies that should be sensitive to the need for uniformity when different courts cannot agree on the interpretation of a rule in the code. New legislation may be incorporated into the code or it may stand alone as statutes. In some jurisdictions such statutes may not carry as much legal weight as the code itself, but generally codes and statutes carry equal weight with the judges. In those nations with constitutions, the constitutions generally establish which one carries more authority if they conflict with any other law except a foreign treaty.

Romano-Germanic law is an old, reliable, and workable system. It is relatively easy for the nonlawyer to find and understand the law in a given area. Judges, who have seen it all and are not likely to be swayed by emotion or sympathy, make most of the decisions. As a result, many consider the process of compensation for damages under Romano-Germanic law fairer to the defense than a system based on a jury trial as in the United States.

Much of the world today has adopted Romano-Germanic law, particularly in the area of regulation of commercial activities. Even the United States with its English traditions, has codified its commercial law to look suspiciously like a Romano-Germanic code.

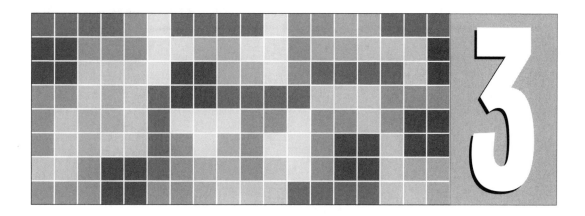

A Tour of the Legal System of England

loser pay

traditional

U.S.

English law has a present-day importance out of proportion to the area to which it originally applied. English law was not, and is not, universally applied in the British Isles. Ireland doesn't use it, neither does the northern part of the Irish isle that is in the United Kingdom. Scotland doesn't use it either. The Channel Islands, and even the Isle of Man, use a different system.

Originally, English law applied only to England and Wales. Today its influence has spread to large areas of the world thanks to the talent of the English to get into ships and travel great distances in order to subjugate large numbers of the world's people.

The influence of English law is found in places alien to the culture of England such as in the laws of India and Pakistan. In a rather pure form it is used in Canada and Australia. English law is the basis of the law used in most of the United States although this law is quite changed from the original version used in England. Even where English law has not been adopted it is sometimes used as a model for revisions in the local system.

English law is unique. It did not evolve from something else in the fashion of Romano-Germanic law. It did not emerge as part of a religion like

Islamic or Hindu-based legal systems. Rather, it developed as a result of a need to unite a nation under an unpopular government.

The story of English law begins about 1,000 years ago with William. He was the illegitimate son of the Duke of Normandy, in part of today's France. When William's father died, a group of nobles attempted to wrest away the dukedom. Through the liberal application of savagery and violence, William crushed the rebellion and assured himself his father's title. Ambition was made of pretty stern stuff in this case, and William was far from satisfied with Normandy.

About this time the king of England, Edward the Confessor, was having some serious in-law problems. Notably, Edward's father-in-law was planning a military campaign against him. Edward enlisted the support of William on the purported promise that William would succeed to the throne. Edward died in 1066 but he did not pass the throne to William. It went to a son of his father-in-law, Harold.

Understandably, William was not happy with this turn of events and decided to take the throne by force. William planned an invasion of England from the South for late summer but bad winds prevented his crossing the channel until September. This delay proved fortuitous to William because the Norwegians invaded from the North just before William's planned invasion. In response Harold took his army up there to meet that invasion. While Harold was busy with the Norwegians, William landed in the South unopposed. Edward succeeded in defeating the Norwegians but his army was weakened by the encounter. When they met the Normans shortly thereafter, William and his army overwhelmed the English. Harold and his brothers were killed in the battle and the way was paved for William to rule England.

The English did not take kindly to the idea of a Norman king. Numerous rebellions protested Norman rule, but William ruthlessly crushed all resistance, often by abundant use of brute force in the South. In the North a different tactic was used. The North was subjugated by the destruction of food stocks and farming implements, thereby bringing about a terrible famine and crushing interest in the rebellion there. Although successful, these tactics were not calculated to win friends and influence people. William had an entire nation under his control, but it hated him and his Normans.

William was not overly concerned with whether he was well liked. He was, however, concerned with keeping control, and so he set up a legal system and government to assist him in that endeavor. He began by dividing England into about 15,000 estates and manors with the idea that no baron of such a small fief could hope to gain enough wealth and power to challenge the king. He also revised the administration of justice.

In feudal times, when most nations were in fact small city-states, the king resolved most disputes personally. The phrase *going to court* originally meant the king's court. Unified England was too big for the king to personally handle all the problems that arose. The king, while unable to hear all the cases, was unwilling, for purposes of maintaining control, to let the local nobles resolve them as was done elsewhere.

England had, from previous times, been divided into 100 counties and the Normans established courts in each one of them. The king appointed the judges. After that, the king did not personally preside as judge over cases unless they were of extreme importance to the kingdom, such as disputes between the nobles, suits involving ownership of land, or serious crimes threatening the peace of the kingdom. Serious crimes are still heard by a court called the King's (or Queen's depending on the gender of the present monarch) Bench. Of course the monarch no longer sits on that bench personally.

Disputes involving ordinary people and daily situations were handled by the county courts. These county courts handled common types of legal disputes for common people and the law they applied was called the common law. Markets and fairs had special courts for commercial disputes, and the church had its own court system for enforcing canon law. Disputes arising from maritime and marine situations were heard in another separate court system called "admiralty courts." All of these courts originally made decisions based on the local tribal customs left over from preconquest days. William recognized and approved the use of tribal customs (or customary law), particularly in the case of small commercial disputes.

Local customs did not, however, cover all situations, and they varied from county to county. A unified nation needed something more complete and standardized. So the judges began to take the liberty to rule on a few new situations. By the end of the thirteenth century, 56 situations in the law required a court to issue an order, called a writ, which put the king's authority on one side or the other in a dispute.

These writs were quite inflexible. The only remedy available for the issuance of a writ was the collection of money damages or return of property. If the case did not fall into one of the 56 situations calling for a writ, no relief could be granted at all. This system, while often not fair, forced the judge to focus on the facts of the case and what solution might achieve justice given those facts, rather than the general principle of law involved. This difference in the focus of the court's attention later defined the common law system.

Although the law remained rigid, the judges of the common law courts noticed patterns in the cases brought before them. And as the population and sophistication of the nation grew, the caseload became more burdensome. From this set of circumstances emerged the principle of precedent.

The setting of precedent allowed the common law to achieve a great deal of precision and consistency, while at the same time reducing the workload for the judges. Suppose the judge had five cases in which a farmer has dammed a creek and denied water to the farm downstream. The judge could hold five separate trials and issue five separate writs ordering the offending farmers to remove the five dams. This solution would be effective, but five trials would be time consuming. The judge's midweek fishing trip would have to be canceled.

As an attractive alternative, the judge could decide the first case and announce publicly that every subsequent case would be decided the same way unless significant differences in the facts were involved. Knowing the outcome in advance, the parties to the other cases would probably settle their dispute without trial, and the judge would be fishing for trout in any of the five disputed creeks by Wednesday.

The common law courts eventually evolved into a pyramid of courts with the largest number of courts, or lower-level courts, conducting trials and making decisions. Above those courts and fewer in number were higher levels of courts. These courts did not conduct trials, but rather reviewed the work of the lower courts to make certain that they had correctly applied the law. A precedent set in one of the appeals courts became the law for all the courts whose appeals came to it. Thus the law became standardized. Anyone could know the disposition of a case under the law by studying how appeals courts had decided a similar case in the past. When an entirely new situation arose, one not covered by precedent, the courts were free to establish a new rule that would be followed until overturned by a higher court or new precedent set from the trial court.

It was vitally important, under this system, to know what courts had done in the past. To facilitate this knowledge of precedents, courts began to keep records of judicial decisions in the seventeenth century. Lawyers and judges could study those records in order to determine the applicable precedent. In the nineteenth century, appeals courts themselves began to publish their decisions in order to make the law clearly understood by the community.

The common law worked well so far as it went, but it was overly rigid. In many situations, it could not result in justice. For example, a contract was valid under common law if it was written, signed by the party sought to be held to it, had a seal on it, and was delivered to the one who sought to enforce it. But what if the signature was obtained by trickery? It was still signed, sealed, and delivered and satisfied the common law test for a valid contract. So although it was based on fraud and was unjust, a common law court would likely recognize and enforce it.

The only recourse for the deceived party was to petition the king, and the king usually referred such matters to his chancellor, a religious man. The chancellor would attempt to resolve the dispute with the application of Christian principles rather than rigid rules of law. In other words, he would determine what a good Christian would do under the circumstances and order the parties to do it. It was said that the common law had only rigid rules and no conscience. Equity law provided the common law with a conscience.

The essence of the chancellor's decisions in such cases over the years evolved into the modern law of equity. Equity law is simply the court's power to order a person or other entity to stop doing something perceived to be wrong, or to order the person or other entity to do something perceived to be right. It is applied where money damages don't quite result in justice.

Suppose you have a new baby in the family but the mother is unable to nurse it. You contract to buy a cow and pay the owner but he fails to deliver it. A common law court would refund your money and perhaps order other money damages to be paid, but that wouldn't keep the baby from starving. Or suppose you needed an additional acre to build a much-needed barn on your farm. An adjoining landowner contracted to sell you one acre at the prevailing price for such acreage. When the time came to close the deal he refused to close the deal. Money damages are not helpful here either, because you haven't really lost anything except the benefit from owning that one particular piece of land. You have not made a payment so there is nothing to refund. The piece of land that you need is unique and no other land would serve as well, and yet you were not exactly cheated out of anything.

A common law court has little to offer in the way of a remedy in either case but an equity court could issue a writ of specific performance that compels the cow owner and adjoining landowner to perform their contracts.

Let us consider another situation. Your neighbor, who does not have a penny to his name, upon awakening each morning, shoots an arrow into your field among your cattle. You have not as yet suffered a loss for money damages from a common law court because no animal has been hit, but eventually you will likely have a loss if the practice continues. Then you could win a common law case, but the neighbor is obviously unable to pay money damages if ordered to do so by a common law court. The remedy in common law is inadequate again, and the solution is to go to a court of equity and seek an injunction, which is an order not to do an act that may cause irreparable harm.

If the neighbor continues shooting after the injunction is issued he will be in contempt of court, meaning he would be in contempt of the king. We have already discussed what sort of fellows these kings were, and nobody really wanted to show contempt for them, at least not without being backed up by a formidable army. Equity, therefore, was and is a powerful weapon in the legal arsenal. A number of specific equitable writs were available from the king's chancellor, and later from special equity courts that took over the job from the chancellor in more recent years.

What if your neighbor's tree is hanging over your house and may fall in the next storm, destroying your house and endangering your family, yet the neighbor refuses to remove it? The remedy is a mandatory injunction that is similar to an injunction except that it is an order to do something rather than to refrain from doing something.

Other aspects of equity law may be used to order a public official to do his duty and are called a writ of mandamus. An example of appropriate use of mandamus could be when a bigoted law enforcement official is ordered to protect innocent victims from a race riot when he has stood by in the past and allowed violence to be used against them.

A number of other remedies compel the restitution of benefits wrongly acquired or the surrender ill-gotten gains. The basic premise of the law of equity is that all wrongs require remedies, and equity steps in if the common law is inadequate for the situation.

Equity does not directly contradict common law. It is applied either where no common law is applicable, or where common law fails to do justice. It orders a party to take an action or refrain from taking an action in a manner that satisfies common law and achieves a just result. For example, if a widow is swindled out of her farm in a way that satisfies common law for a legal conveyance of real estate, the equity court will order the swindler to sign a deed conveying it back to the widow in a manner also consistent with common law. Thus the authority of the king is not pitted against that of the church directly. The wrongdoer is simply ordered to take actions under the common law, undoing the wrong that had no remedy under common law. The phrase used was "equity follows the law." England maintained a separate court system to apply the laws of equity until the nineteenth century.

Prior to the nineteenth century, English law was primarily formed by judges acting under authority of the monarchy. As England democratized, legislation from the parliament became an important source of law, and the law was reorganized.

The separate equity courts were eventually consolidated with the common law courts, and all English courts subsequently applied both common law and equity. Court decisions, however, remained the most definitive source of English law, and no attempt was made to codify the entire body of law.

No efforts sought to make the law of England rational and logical either. English law was not formed in universities, and it was not formed by legislators who were attempting to create an organized body of law as was done in Romano-Germanic jurisdictions on the continent. Rather, individual judges, dealing with practical problems one at a time, formed the common law and equity. These judges were usually not university educated but were trained in an apprentice-like setting, working for a judge or lawyer and studying under the supervision of a mentor.

Although the ancient Romans and Greeks conducted various forms of jury trials, the English, for a time, made jury trials an integral part of their legal system. Henry II, who ruled late in the twelfth century, began the custom of using ordinary citizens to decide civil cases. Henry did not use juries to decide guilt in criminal cases because that method was thought to be the prerogative of the king, but he did appoint 12 citizens to report to him about the crimes thought to have been committed so that the King's Bench could try them. This practice was the beginning of the modern grand jury, which indicts, or accuses, but does not determine guilt.

By the nineteenth century a jury untrained in law decided many types of English trials. This format required that strict rules of evidence be developed so that the jury would see only evidence that would fairly advance the case in one direction or another. Evidence that would be ignored by a judge as having nothing to do with the case, such as allegations of obnoxious behavior on the part of a farmer involved in a boundary dispute, might wrongly sway a jury. Consequently such irrelevant testimony was barred from admission into a trial. The use of juries resulted in strict and detailed rules of evidence in English law jurisdictions. In recent years the use of juries has declined in England but the strict rules of evidence remain.

One rather profound difference between English and Romano-Germanic courts is that English courts often utilize open court hearings where both sides are invited to present their testimony and oral arguments. This practice also stemmed from the English use of the jury system. In previous times most juries were illiterate; that fact required different procedures from those used in Romano-Germanic jurisdictions.

In the Romano-Germanic system, where the jurists were most often educated in universities, a court decision could be made on the basis of a file of documents and affidavits submitted by the parties. Cases had little need for a "day in court" in the form of an oral trial.

In the English system an illiterate jury had to make a decision based on what they could hear and see as opposed to what they could read. Therefore, the disputes were usually reduced to a series of yes-or-no questions or choosing some amount of money. When a dispute arose, a trial was held where both sides, through use of physical evidence, testimony, and oral arguments, tried to persuade the jury to answer the questions in a favorable way.

Once the trial began the jury was, of necessity, protected from influence by being sequestered away from the public. While sequestered, the jury members were not free to pursue other matters and were greatly inconvenienced, so it was important that the trial proceed without undue delay. When the evidence and arguments were concluded the jury rendered the verdict quickly so that the jury members could be liberated to go about their normal business.

The concept of contempt of court still plays a large part in the English legal system. In many Romano-Germanic jurisdictions, it is difficult to execute a judgment once it is rendered. The losing defendant in a lawsuit may not be required to disclose his or her income or assets and public authorities may refuse to assist in collecting judgments. Such is not the case under English law. Any disregard of court orders given under English law often results in imprisonment until full compliance is forthcoming.

Doing business under the English legal system is, in some respects, easier but in some other respects, more difficult than under other European legal systems. If one has a complicated legal problem it is unlikely that one will find a clear answer in the codes of Romano-Germanic systems.

Individual judges may interpret the fine principles of a situation differently. So an element of uncertainty surrounds how the law is likely to affect business based on the judge's interpretation. The answer to the question "Are we legal or not?" may depend on the judge's viewpoint or whether the judge is sympathetic.

The English system, by contrast, has been around for 1,000 years, and decisions made under it have generally been followed in subsequent cases. It is probable that in all those years a set of circumstances similar to the present case has been adjudicated, and it is generally safe to assume that whatever decision was rendered in the former case will be rendered again in the present one, absent contravening legislation.

The problem with English law is that even if the legal problem is not a complex one, the lawyers must still look through 1,000 years of cases to determine the exact nature of the law. In the Romano-Germanic system of law, one would quickly find the answer to a simple legal question in the form of an exact provision in one of just a few volumes of organized code.

The English system is entirely workable and business has prospered under it for many centuries. It is particularly difficult for someone accustomed to the Romano-Germanic system to negotiate the English system, however, and expert advice is essential.

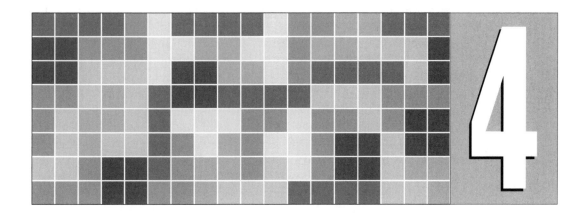

A Tour of the Law of the United States

The beginning point for the study of the law in the United States is the English legal system. Although the Dutch and Swedish, as well as the English, founded the original colonies of the United States, all the colonies were English by 1664 and none but the English had a profound influence on colonial law. In a case decided in 1608, the English courts ruled that English people carried English law with them wherever they settled, and therefore English law applied to the people living in the American colonies.

English law, however, was specific to English conditions. Luckily one wise passage in the court's opinion stated that English law would be applied "so far as it was adapted to institutions and circumstances" in the new colonies. So the colonies started with English law, but also had a free hand to make it work in the New World. It was fortunate that this proviso was included. For its time, English law was well developed and technical, incorporating intricate procedures. But the New World of the seventeenth century was almost completely devoid of trained lawyers and judges. Life and commerce were primitive, and conditions were nothing like those that fostered the development of the common law. Common law had been originally developed for a feudal society, which was unlike the conditions that existed among the colonists in the New World. In fact, life in America was notably different from anywhere in Europe, and the colonists faced many new problems not contemplated by the common law.

Even if English common law had been adapted to the American scene, many colonists were not eager to submit to English law in any case. Many colonists had immigrated to the colonies precisely in order to escape religious persecution, debtors' prisons, political problems, or other perceived injustices of England. They didn't want to be followed to America by England's hated institutions. Even if they had been willing to use English law verbatim, few in the colonies knew anything about it.

The earliest laws in the new colonies were not English laws therefore, but legal decisions based on the Bible or lists of rules prepared by the colonial communities. Both of these forms of law are more similar to laws passed by a legislature (called statutes) and codes than English common law. In the legal system of the United States, statute law and codes were much more readily accepted than they had been in England.

The common law got a boost in the eighteenth century when England and its American colonies were united against a common enemy. The English presence in America was challenged by those in New France, that is, Canada and Louisiana. The enemy did not distinguish between English-speaking colonists or those people from England itself. With England a helpful ally in the face of this grave security threat, English institutions were, for a period, more readily accepted and American courts began to pay more attention to English law.

By the end of the eighteenth century, however, everything had changed. The former colonies were now a new, independent nation. The French threat had disappeared. Canada was taken over by England in 1763, and the new United States absorbed Louisiana in a cash deal with the French in 1803.

After the revolution against England, several states of the new American nation banned the use of English law in their courts. Because of hard feelings left by the war, anything English was, for a time, viewed unfavorably. The Americans considered the British government to be a thoroughly undesirable institution. In their rejection of things British they set about to design a republic organized around a constitution and a bill of rights. These documents looked a lot like Romano-Germanic codes and nothing like an English monarchy. By this time the new republic was allied with France and some states of the nation toyed with the idea of adopting something like the French code that was already in use in the new territory of Louisiana.

Adding to the pressure to use code law, Texas and California joined the union. Both had traditions of using the Spanish code that was Romano-Germanic in character. The waves of immigrants from nations such as Ireland, which were code jurisdictions, did not particularly relish anything English. By the beginning of the nineteenth century, a groundswell of support pushed for the adoption of a general code to be used as the body of law for the United States.

Court, which generally hears cases of great importance, usually with great constitutional issues involved. No right of appeal is afforded to cases of the U.S. Supreme Court. It hears only the cases it deems important enough for its attention.

Depending on the size of the state, states generally have two or three levels of courts. States with three levels mimic the federal system with trial courts, courts of appeals, and a final highest court, called a supreme court in most, but not all, states.

If any party demands it, juries decide questions of fact in nearly all U.S. courts. Although little used in modern English courts, the right of access to a jury trial is guaranteed by the U.S. constitution's Seventh Amendment for cases involving more than $20. No right of a jury trial is offered in cases that invoke only the law of equity or in cases where the facts are not in dispute. This right to a jury trial has advantages and disadvantages for business litigants. The jury generally removes bias from the trial because the jury is selected at the time of trial from disinterested citizens who represent a cross-section of the community. The disadvantage of a jury trial is that the jury may not be equipped to understand or deal objectively with a case involving complex law or technical issues.

American courts, like their English counterparts, set precedent with their decisions, but U.S. courts do not preserve precedent as steadfastly as their English counterparts. Precedent is merely followed until it is overturned, and U.S. courts do not hesitate to overturn precedent if the times have changed or if the politics of the court have changed. Oftentimes precedent is overturned in state courts because a majority of the other states have adopted a different precedent and the state wishes to be in conformance with the majority. The businessperson should be aware of this constant flux in U.S. common law and not consider that the present interpretation of common law will last forever.

Most business activities in the United States involve aspects regulated by either or both federal or state laws. It is easier to search and understand the application of federal law. Federal law is mostly codified and can be found in published form in the U.S. Code. The law cannot be understood, however, without an examination of the cases that have been decided under each provision of the code. These decisions are found in the various published volumes called *reporters*. The same holds true for state courts. To be of assistance in this search, legal digests summarize cases in each area of law, and legal encyclopedias describe the general principles of each area of law. Legal research in the United States is quite difficult and, if done by an amateur, is fraught with peril. Considering the large awards of damages rendered in the United States for those who are perceived to injure or violate the rights of a plaintiff, understanding one's obligations under U.S. law is best left to the professional.

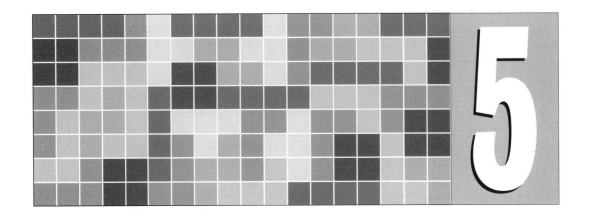

A Tour of the Law of Islamic Nations

The word *Islam* conjures up images of an alien and hostile culture in many western minds, but such images often belie the truth. It is not especially difficult to do business under the Islamic legal system, but the Islamic system is unique. Working with the Islamic legal system requires a special frame of mind, and Islamic law can only be understood if one understands something of the religion itself.

It is important to have some concept of how the Islamic system works, if only because such a large part of the world is dominated by or influenced by it. More than 30 of the world's nations are predominantly Muslim. They range from the Atlantic to the Pacific and some are hugely populous. They stretch from the Atlantic coast of Northern Africa, across the center of Asia and the Indian subcontinent, and continue all the way to Indonesia in the Pacific. Even though popular association matches Islam with Arabia, Arabs account for less than a fifth of Muslims. In fact, most Muslims live east of the Arabian Peninsula.

Islam's greatest difference with other legal systems is the source of its law. Although religion influences the course of many legal systems, specific laws are normally enacted by the law-making agents of secular governments, be it a king, parliament, regulatory agency, or other. In other words, laws originate with people in most of the world. In those parts of the world, people have the power to change the laws as deemed necessary from time to time.

In countries that have adopted the Islamic legal system, no person, indeed no power on Earth, has the authority to make a law. Laws are thought to be prescribed for humankind directly by God, and all people are subject to the law. To claim the authority to make a law is to claim to be a god, which is absolutely forbidden.

Law in Islamic countries comes directly from the religion, so to explain the law one must first explain the religion. Hence, a brief discussion of Islam follows.

Islam begins with the prophet Abraham and has the same roots as Judaism. A Muslim is required to submit to the will of God. Islam means "submission" in Arabic. The will of God is said to have been revealed to humans through a long list of prophets, beginning with Abraham and continuing with a list of names familiar to Jews and Christians. The names Ishmael, Moses, David, and Jesus are familiar to Muslims. However, Jesus is considered to be only another in this line of prophets. Muslims revere Jesus but do not recognize the special relation of Jesus to God that Christians envision.

The last prophet in the line is Mohammed who filled in all the remaining blanks by revealing the holy book, the Quran (known to Westerners as the Koran). Quran is the final authority in Islam on the subject of God's intentions for humans on Earth.

Islamic law was developed in the Middle Ages and is completely based on religious principles. It is a nonrational legal system that comes from theology rather than reasoning. It is believed to be divinely inspired and, unlike any other legal system, is based entirely on the Quran.

Islamic law is quite unique among legal systems in the sense that it is considered to come directly from God. By contrast, it contains no Christian law. Christians were instructed to respect the secular law of the place where they were living and keep their faith separate from government. (Christ is deemed to have said: "Render unto Caesar that which is Caesar's and to God that which is God's" and "My Kingdom is not of this world.") Christian canon law is generally not considered by Christians to be divinely inspired, and it is not designed to replace governmental law. Indeed Christians may violate an unjust law and not expect to be punished in any afterlife for doing so. Islam, by contrast, expressly incorporates law in the religion and violation of Islamic law might subject the violator to punishment in the next world.

In the tenth century Islamic scholars decided that the law was complete and no changes would ever be revealed by God. This decision effectively froze the legal system in the Middle Ages and has lead to monumental problems in adapting the system to the modern world.

The Quran, like the Bible, is not specific on what should be done in various situations that one encounters in living a human life. It does have

some firm rules in about 80 of its more than 6,000 verses, such as a requirement for the complete avoidance of alcohol and gambling, but em-
bellishments are lacking. The Quran serves only as the framework for Islamic
law. It is not detailed enough to serve as a legal system for commercial purposes. For example, the Quran forbids the use of alcohol, but it does not
specify whether it is prohibited to buy and sell alcohol as part of a commercial activity, remain friends with those who drink alcohol, or sell raw
materials and equipment for the production of alcohol.

One method of defining answers to this type of question is the study of
the life of the prophet Mohammed himself. He is deemed by Muslims to
have led a perfect life, and written accounts of his actions survive. Therefore
it is considered possible to study the decisions and actions that he made
during his lifetime and thereby gain insight into how he might have be-
haved in some modern but parallel situation. The story of Mohammed's life
is called the Sunna.

Another source of Islamic law has been the treatises of Islamic scholars
called fiqh. At one time the fiqh were a basic source of Islamic law, but because of many conflicts between them the fiqh have largely fallen into dis-
use except in Saudi Arabia.

Another source of Islamic law, in wider use today, is the consensus of Islamic judges who institutionalized accepted principles of law. This formation of law happened as a result of lengthy debates on various legal subjects
where agreements were reached throughout a wide range of the Islamic
world. This traditional Islamic law is called Ijima.

The modern world has presented Islam with a host of new legal situations not addressed in the simple law of a simple society. How should the
law deal with allocation of the radio bandwidth? What is the remedy for a
loss due to an airplane crash? What is an electronic medical device does not
perform as represented? These questions were obviously not at issue in the
situations presented in the life of Mohammed or his contemporaries. Islam
follows four approaches to such a problem.

1. **Ijtihad.** With this doctrine, a scholar is permitted to solve a legal problem when no precedent is to be found. Ijtihad has fallen from favor because some Islamic scholars believe that it is sometimes used to
   substitute the will of the jurist for the word of God.

2. **Qiyas.** These parallels are drawn between old law sources and applied
   to modern situations. Does the law established in the Middle Ages for a
   horse and cart apply to the same situation involving a pickup truck?
   Under this doctrine, an Islamic jurist may decide a case in a new situation if a similarity can be drawn between it and an established principle.

3. **Al-Istihsan.** Islamic jurists in some jurisdictions are free to have a conscience and do the right thing. If Islamic law is not clear, they may make
   a decision considering public and private interests and the desire to

avoid improper results. A decision made by generally applying Islamic principles is called Al-Istihsan. Not every Islamic jurisdiction recognizes the right of a judge to use this approach. In fact, most conservative jurisdictions do not.

4. **Urf.** Like all societies, Islamic lands have developed local customs that define the accepted business or social practice in many areas. Islamic courts in some jurisdictions give such long-standing customs and practice the force of law. This practice is known as Urf.

The entire body of Islamic law is knows as Sharia which means "the way" or literally the "path to water." Answers to all questions about proper Islamic conduct, including legal ones, should be found somewhere in the Sharia.

Most Islamic courts consist of a *Qadi* who makes the decision and *Mufti* who are experts on Islamic law and who advise the Qadi. A legal decision handed down by such a court is a *fatwa*.

The evidence accepted by an Islamic court usually consists of witnesses' oral testimony. Prima facie proof requires either the testimony of two men or one man and two women. An admission, or refusal to take an oath before God denying the claim, is also considered proof. The Qadi selects witnesses and the possibility exists that he may choose witnesses who are fellow Muslims and therefore perhaps favor a Muslim party.

ADVICE TO THE TRAVELER

Although it is not the general purpose of this text to cover legal topics other than those directly related to business, the reader of this book is likely to be involved in foreign assignments. Because human nature is what it is, the reader should understand the consequences of romance in the Islamic context.

Islam forbids a Muslim woman to marry a non-Muslim man; marriage of a Muslim woman requires the consent of a male relative or guardian.

A Muslim man may marry a non-Muslim woman who is from another Abrahamic people (i.e., Christians and Jews), but the new wife is expected to embrace Islam after the marriage. A Muslim man may not marry a non-Abrahamic woman. Divorce can take place by oral declaration of the husband, mutual agreement, or fatwa. A husband who utters his divorce declaration during the heat of an argument may change his mind during a waiting period before the divorce becomes effective. A divorced woman also has a waiting period before she is free to remarry.

Extramarital sexual relations carry extreme penalties under Islamic law as interpreted in some countries. The woman's father or guardian, in order to prevent a smear on the family honor, may legally murder a female who commits unchaste acts in many Islamic countries.

Adoption of children is forbidden by Islam, and therefore by law, in all Islamic nations except Tunisia.

ISLAMIC COMMERCIAL LAW

Islamic law differs from traditional western legal systems in several areas of substantive commercial law. Some areas that are likely to bushwhack a foreign businessperson include the following:

- Islamic philosophy generally considers knowledge to be the common heritage of mankind and does not encourage the protection of intellectual property such as patents, trademarks, trade secrets, and logos. In the process of joining the wider commercial world, this philosophy has been subjugated in some cases to the need to conform to the expectations of the rest of the world. Some legislation has been enacted since the 1960s to promote protection of intellectual property, particularly with respect to the rights of authors.

- Islamic law forbids gambling, and "gambling" is interpreted to mean many types of contracts involving reward for the taking of risks. Some jurisdictions do not draw a distinction between gambling and insurance, hence the avoidance of risk through an insurance policy is forbidden. Strict Sharia jurisdictions may forbid mortgages as a form of gambling on the possibility of repayment. Many prohibit futures trading or speculative share trading on the same basis.

- The Quran expressly forbids the charging of interest in an unfair way. Some Islamic jurisdictions consider all interest unfair, others consider only excessive interest to be prohibited. As a practical matter, this Islamic doctrine does not negate the universally accepted economic principle that possession of money has a value based on time. Several strategies have developed to circumvent this prohibition. The result is that interest is actually being charged, but it is not called interest. For example, a bank may periodically share its profits with its depositors. Another ruse may be the transfer of some real estate to a lender in place of money interest. Or two sales may take place instead of one in order to add the interest differential. In this scheme, the lender buys the property from the seller for a lower price and sells it to the real buyer for a higher price that is to be paid in the future. Unfortunately, in international transactions, such fictions may result in double transfer taxes.

- Muslims must fulfill their contracts. Contracts under Islamic law are formed in the usual way with an offer followed by an acceptance and a meeting of the minds. Islamic courts will enforce a contract that is legal under Islamic law regardless of the religion of the parties, however they will not do so before a debtor who is in serious economic straits has had a chance to recover. Not every Islamic country applies Sharia contract law. Bahrain has adopted much of English commercial law while Iraq and Kuwait have civil codes similar to European (i.e., Romano-Germanic) civil law.

- Be wary of initiating negotiations that you do not intend to complete when subject to Islamic legal jurisdiction. One glaring difference between Muslim and other types of legal systems is the concept of pre-contractual liability. Under most of the world's legal systems, neither negotiating party has any liability whatsoever until a contract is formed. The parties may freely withdraw from the negotiations at any stage up to that point. Under Islamic law a party is obliged to bargain in good faith once negotiations are entered. If ongoing negotiations are simply terminated by one party, the other party may be entitled to compensation. This entitlement is terminated with respect to the seller if the buyer withdraws because he discovers that the goods are defective.

- Islamic law is also restrictive of a contract's parties' freedom to name their own terms. The Sharia prescribes or proscribes certain terms for all contracts, such as the restriction on charging interest.

- An offer may be revoked by the offeror before the offeree receives it. An acceptance may be likewise revoked by the offeree or rejected by the offeror before it reaches the offeror.

- Sellers must honestly describe their goods. The Sharia prohibits telling falsehoods. If the seller does so, the buyer may rescind the contract without consequence.

- Islamic law does not permit one to unjustly enrich himself or herself, and this theory is applied to the seller's silence on relevant information about the goods. If the information is not critical, the seller is not required to disclose information about the goods that the seller is not asked about. However, if the omission is so blatant and the information so important to the contract that not making the disclosure constitutes fraud, an Islamic court may find unjust enrichment and award compensation to the buyer. For example, the buyer of a new car is entitled to expect that it will be delivered with an engine installed and would probably be compensated by the courts if he received his new car without one, even though he did not ask whether the car came with one. But he may not expect a full tank of gasoline unless he specifically asked whether it was included and was promised it was.

- Parties are not bound by their contracts under the Islamic system if unpredictable circumstances arise that would destroy the fundamental fairness of the agreement. For example a lease may be rescinded if the lessor loses his job and must seek employment elsewhere. And performance may be excused if performance of a contract becomes much more difficult that anticipated. For example, consider a contract to make an ocean delivery to a given area by a certain date two weeks in the future. This contract could be rescinded if a hurricane moves into the area.

- Most governments do not allow themselves to be sued. This refusal is based on the long-standing international law doctrine of sovereign immunity. Islamic law does not recognize such a doctrine, and government contractors can expect the protection of the legal system against the government just as if they were dealing with a private party.

Although Islamic law is alien to western-trained businesspeople, it is a functioning legal system. Many opportunities exist in the Islamic world and the businessperson should not be discouraged by the legal system from pursuing them. The situation simply requires a bit more caution and expert advice.

A Tour of the Law of India

One might expect to find some similarities between India and the United States. After all, both were British colonies, both are multi-ethnic, and both are federations of states, but obviously they are not the same. When more than a billion people, in a culture thousands of years old, live in an area one-third the size of the United States, and 34 percent of them are under the age of 14, one might expect a radically different culture and legal system in spite of the aforementioned similarities. In India such expectations are realized.

Being a land with a mixture of Hinduism, Islam, and English law and culture, India is a complex society for the Westerner to understand. Although it is a poor county with gross domestic product per capital of just under U.S. $2000, the country is so populous that the numbers extrapolate to nearly a $2 trillion economy.

To understand law in present-day India one must also understand something of India's history and something of the Hindu religion. India's history could be the subject of volumes by itself, but we shall be mercifully brief in this text.

India is one of the timeless places of the earth. Evidence of human habitation has been found dating back half a million years. Fortunately, we don't have to go back that far to understand the legal system. Two events took place about 3,000 years ago that provide us with a good starting point for this chapter.

The first was the development of the caste system. About 1500 B.C. invaders from what is present-day Iran conquered India. These people, called Aryans, had developed a system of social classes called Varnas. One's Varna was permanently set by the Varna of one's parents.

The Varna was supposed to have been earned by the type of existence the individual lived in a previous life and a change could only take place in the next life. This ultimate manifestation of social stratification is the antithesis of the concept that all humans are equal. This system, called the caste system, dictates that humans are created unequally and the level at which one is created can never be changed in this lifetime. Race and occupation originally determined one's caste and it was an immutable birthright, or curse. Each person was a member of the social class the person was born into . . . **period.** Personal achievements and accumulated wealth are irrelevant to this measure of a person's stature. This philosophy is deeply ingrained into Hindu culture and religion. Although originally passed orally from generation to generation, the rules for caste and other matters were written down about 1000 B.C. into a compilation known as the Laws of Manu. Aside from defining the caste system the Laws of Manu suggested the proper course of action for dealing with legal problems ranging from contracts to criminal matters. The Laws of Manu remain the basis of Hindu law in India.

Hindus believe, and the Law of Manu dictates, that a person's previous life determines that person's lot in this life, and the position born into in this life cannot be changed. If one lives a good life one may be reincarnated into a better caste the next time one lives, but for present one stays where one is.

The Four primary castes are called Varnas. At the bottom is a fifth class, the Dalits, who have no social status at all, in essence, no Varna. These hapless ones are commonly known as the untouchables. These people are condemned by Hinduism to live by menial labor outside the social mainstream of society. At the top of the castes are the Brahmins who are the priestly elite. Next are the Kshatriya or warrior class followed by the merchants and farmers known as the Vaisya. At the bottom of those with caste are the servants and artisans who are the Shudras. The categories are made up of more than 2,000 subclasses.

Legally speaking, discrimination based on the caste system has been abolished in India since 1950, and in the cities the cruelty of the caste system seems to have lessened to some degree. In the villages and rural areas it is also illegal but still very much alive, and the visitor must be careful about the social implications of personal associations.

Modern India has initiated an affirmative action program with certain numbers of government jobs and other positions reserved for lower caste or no-caste individuals. This policy has resulted in tensions between the castes as members of the higher castes react to perceived discrimination against them.

Those who react with moral outrage in the West against the caste system are quite correct, but before they become too judgmental they should recall the institution of black slavery in the American South or debtors' prisons of Europe. One will find enough inhumanity to go around.

The second legacy of the Aryans that shaped modern India was the foundation of the religion that evolved into Hinduism. The foundation of Hinduism is the oral tradition of the Vedas. The Vedas, which include an elaborate system of mythology, describe a ritualistic form of worshiping a plethora of the Aryans. They were seminomadic tribes who left little behind except their contribution to the culture.

Four major religions have developed in India. They are Hinduism, Sikhism, Buddhism, and Jainism. Today, about 2 percent of Indians are Sikhs. Although Buddhism flourished outside of India, it is practiced by less than 1 percent of the people in the land of its birth place. The number of Jain is insignificant. The second largest religion in India is Islam. Large numbers of Muslims remained in India after the division of Pakistan and Bangladesh; they comprise about 12 percent of the present population. The third largest is Christianity with about 2.5 percent. Judaism arrived in India before it arrived in Europe; and India still has a few thousand Jews. The rest, and the vast majority of Indians, are Hindus. Of these religions only Hinduism and Islam have had any significant effect on the legal system.

Historically, the next great event in India after the Aryan domination was its slow conquest and unification by a succession of Muslim invaders. Prior to the Muslim invasions, India was a disjointed collection of kingdoms. Arabs penetrated militarily into India about A.D. 700. Over the succeeding centuries, wave after wave of Turks, Afghans, Persians, and Mongols chipped away at the Indian subcontinent establishing a series of sultanates until Babur, a Persian, united the entire area in a glorious empire called the Mogul dynasty. United under Islamic rule, India produced Akbar, one of its greatest rulers during this period of the Mogul dynasty. Akbar promoted religious tolerance and a sense of Indian unity, which was a new idea in the sixteenth century India. Had subsequent rulers followed Akbar's example, India might be quite different today. Unfortunately they did not, and the Moguls who followed Akbar attempted to suppress Hinduism, which resulted in divisions that eventually weakened the Mogul empire and served as an invitation for European powers to fill the vacuum.

In the seventeenth centuries both the British and French attempted to establish colonies in India in the form of private trading companies. The British East India company squared off against the French East India company in a privately operated military conflict during the Seven Years' War of 1761. The British company won the battle and the right to do business

in, and govern, much of India. The British were to rule India until the middle
of the twentieth century.

India received its independence from the United Kingdom in a fairly
peaceful revolt under the leadership of the Indian National Congress
headed by Mahatma Gandhi shortly after the end of the Second World War.
Gandhi's campaign of passive resistance coupled with economic boycotts
was a novelty but quite effective in India where the protestors outnumbered
their colonial masters by thousands to one. At that time the national territory included what is today Pakistan and Bangladesh. When independence
was achieved the commitment to nonviolence ended abruptly. Between
each other, the citizens of the new India vigorously initiated brutal warfare
to establish who would dominate the new government.

This political violence was particularly pronounced between the Hindu
and Muslim factions of Indian society. The solution finally achieved was the
division of some of the northeastern and northwestern segments (i.e., Pakistan
and Bangladesh), where Islamic governments were allowed to dominate, and
Islamic law applies today.

Hindus dominated the rest of India, which kept the name of the former
whole, though it retained some population of Muslims, Sikhs, and Christians. This decision to divide India was not popular among many Hindus
who felt that they should dominate all of former colonial India. The archi-
tect of independence, Mahatma Gandhi, the great advocate of nonviolence,
was labeled a traitor and assassinated for agreeing to the split.

The conflict between Muslims and Hindus continues to this day with
regular border skirmishes and four full-scale wars between India and Pakistan
over the years. Both sides have armed themselves with nuclear weapons in
their own version of the cold war.

In this book we are concerned with the Hindu-dominated nation that
is present-day India. Pakistan and Bangladesh, now having Islamic legal systems, are covered in a different chapter of this book.

Hindu law comes from its religious principles as set forth in sacred texts
known as the Scrutis. The Scrutis have been lost through the years and only
small fragments survive. Consequently treatises called the sastras govern
Hindu life. Of the three sastras, two deal with government and pleasure seeking. The third, the dharma, teaches about how to prosper and is of the most
interest to the business community. The dharma is not a law book in a strict
sense but it does describe how business fits in the order of the universe and
sets forth a businessperson's duties. Like other Eastern religions, no reference
is made to rights. The dharmas are not considered to be divine in origin,
but are written by men and have entered the realm of tradition. If no
dharma principle or local custom applies, the dharma requires a decision
to be made on the basis of conscience. Under Hindu tradition, precedents
and legislation are not binding because the government should be free to
adopt a better principle in the future should one come along. The dharma,
along with local customs, is the basis of Hindu commercial law.

The dharma is not law in the sense of western law; the only sanctions it sets forth are loss of caste and social standing. Nevertheless, English courts applied dharma principles to make decisions on liability. They then imposed English legal sanctions when making decisions on commercial disputes in India and in that way Hindu customs assumed the force of law. During the time of Muslim domination of India, Hindu law was not applied at all by governments although the people kept their Hindu customs. When the English replaced the Moguls they decided to avoid unrest by having their courts apply Hindu principles to disputes. For the first time, this gave old Hindu customs the force of law with courts to enforce it. However, it was extremely difficult for English courts to understand or apply the Sastras, so the judges used local Hindu experts, called pandits, to interpret Hindu law for them. Often the English court was a mere rubber stamp for the decision of the pandits. In North India some attempt was made to translate and codify Hindu law so English judges could apply it directly while in the South the pandit system remained.

The English had the effect of standardizing Hindu law, looking as they were, at larger areas of India rather than the unique local customs of each village. The British were, however, reluctant to do much legislation in India for fear of offending the religious sensibilities of the populace and sparking a revolt, but they did begin legislative overtures to end the caste system and the live cremation of widows, practices they found abhorrent. Further legislation was enacted codifying the Hindu law of inheritance and wills. Eventually Hindu law was applied to marriage, inheritance, and the institutions of religion, but English law was increasingly applied in commercial areas.

After its independence, India continued the process of standardizing and codifying Hindu law. The constitution drawn up after independence promised retention of English law where colonial courts and codification of Hindu law applied it. It abolished the caste system. So English influence over the law continued even with the absence of the English. Today, India continues to apply common law in many areas of life and is developing its own common law.

Indian courts set precedent today and the Supreme Court sets precedent over the entire nation. The Supreme Court's ability to set precedent is guaranteed by the constitution. India has also retained the English-style court system. A change in the law is not necessarily a change in the thoughts and attitudes of people with 3,000 years of tradition though, and many of the legally forbidden customs continue in the villages.

Since independence a movement has sought to replace Hindu law with a national law of India that would be independent of religion. These efforts are worth watching. They could portend a commercial code similar to those used in the West, and make business in India easier for foreigners.

As it stands India adopted a constitution in 1950 that guarantees many of the rights found in the U.S. Constitution. Speech, expression, and assembly are guaranteed. Citizens are protected against state power in criminal matters as well. The Supreme Court may subject police power and legislative action to judicial review.

The constitution outlaws the caste system, but caste remains a social reality in Indian society. Frequent reports suggest that Dalits still are sometimes subjected to extreme discrimination and violence. They are routinely assigned the most menial jobs available. India has established an affirmative action program for the lower castes but most still live humiliating lives of poverty. In the literature about doing business in India, foreign businesspersons are cautioned that to hire a lower-caste person as a salesperson is likely to result in stymied sales to higher castes who may refuse to deal with a low-caste person or a Dalit.

The law used in India today is a combination of the national constitution, which has a U.S.-style bill of rights, Hindu law as modified by British courts (particularly used in the areas of family law and inheritance), legislation introduced by the British before independence, legislation passed by the Indian parliament after independence, and English common law. The Indian parliament uses new English statutes for models in adopting new legislation so Indian statutory law, in many respects, is similar to British law.

Indian tort law with respect to foreign investors has recently been clarified by litigation arising from the Bhopal chemical gas disaster. This matter involved an Indian corporation partially owned by a U.S. corporation, which had an accident that resulted in the deaths of thousands of people. The state of the law seems to be that there is an absolute duty on the part of companies engaged in hazardous activities to pay damages when they injure someone, but such damages are limited to what the courts normally award against an Indian company. Such awards tend to be small, and so the Indian government has tried to assure foreign investors that it will not bankrupt them if an accident occurs in India.

Business was hampered in India for many years by the Indian courts' refusal to honor awards made as a result of arbitration. Private business often considers litigation in court to be too slow and expensive to be the primary dispute resolution mechanism in the commercial world. Consequently, most businesses put arbitration clauses into routine contracts so private panels, applying simple procedures, can decide such disputes. Courts in most nations in the world respect decisions of arbitration panels, but India did not until 1996. Before that time, India permitted a losing party in an arbitration proceeding to appeal to the courts, a process that could take as long as 15 years, which effectively defeated the purpose of arbitration. The deficiency in Indian law has thankfully been corrected.

Until 1991 Indian law was not conducive to foreign investment. Many industries were prohibited to foreigners, others required special government permission, and technology transfer was strictly regulated. Restrictions hampered the use of foreign brand names in India, Indian currency was not convertible, import duties were high, and capital markets were tightly regulated.

India had a poor reputation for the protection of intellectual property as well. The result was a strangulation of India's development. By 1997, legislation or adoption of international intellectual property treaties addressed all of these problems. Some seem to be solved, but others were addressed by half measures. India now has a national policy of actively seeking and encouraging foreign investment in order to improve the economy. Unfortunately its policy of acquiring nuclear weapons and continuing a dangerous standoff with Pakistan runs counter to this intention.

India offers the foreign investor a familiar legal system, liberalized investment laws, and a large English-speaking population with low wage levels. India suffers from a reputation of having a contradictory and corrupt government, as well as insufficient infrastructure for many types of industry. India has come a long way but has more work to do.

A Tour of the Law of China

China has been an important nation for more than 3,000 years. For most of that period it was the foremost nation in the world by almost every measurement. Unfortunately for China, the West industrialized first and China's premier status was lost in the nineteenth century. When China lost its edge, the West did not hesitate to use its superior military power to impose its will on China. In the nineteenth and early twentieth centuries, the western powers imposed an "open door" policy on China giving nearly everyone a voice in China except the Chinese.

This domination by the West was a relatively short period considering the total historical record of China, but the epoch was humiliating and brutal. One of the worst humiliations occurred in the middle of the nineteenth century when the British successfully prosecuted two military campaigns against China. Their purpose was to protect the British practice of selling opium in China over the vehement objections of the Chinese government. The Chinese were morally outraged over this trade. The British traffic in opium created millions of pathetic addicts.

The Chinese view of the outside world was greatly and adversely affected by this time of western domination and, until recently, the Chinese were reluctant to accept anything of western culture, including a western legal system.

China had a tumultuous beginning of the twentieth century during which time it was occupied by a number of powers and finally invaded by Japan. The departure of the foreign powers after the Second World War left a power vacuum and rivalry among competing ideologies, which sparked a civil war. Eventually, China stabilized to some extent with the establishment, by force of arms, of the People's Republic. This repressive Communist government imposed strict controls over the economy and political expression.

In recent years China has been perceived as an economic and military threat to the West. At first glance, China might appear to be too poor and weak to be of consequence, but any country nearly the size of the United States, with more than a billion people, and possessing nuclear weapons cannot and should not be ignored.

The incompetence of the Communist politicians who managed the centrally planned economy during the early part of its communist experience is legendary. China made little economic progress until a succession in power in 1978 led to needed economic liberalization. Since then China has enjoyed a period of relative prosperity although political controls on the populace are still entirely in the hands of the Communist party and have been harsh and violently repressive.

China, however, has never been a country to tolerate dissent and tumult, nor does it tolerate the rule of law as we know it in the West. Therefore, before we take a look at the law of China we should be aware of the diminished role of law in that country.

In the West, law seems all-important. We eagerly seek favorable changes in legislation. The decision to file a lawsuit is often made on a purely economic basis. We may not hesitate to involve the force of the law and the police power of the state in a situation if we perceive that such intervention could bring us some benefit. The law is conceived to be a force for good, bringing peace and justice to the world. Chinese consider the force of law to be the opposite.

In China, and much of the Far East, philosophy is greatly influenced by the thoughts of an ancient judge named Confucius. Although Confucius lived 500 years before the time of Christ, his rules, designed to smooth the relations between members of society, permeate all aspects of Chinese life. All through Chinese history, and today, his ideas have profoundly affected the legal system.

In a word, Confucian philosophy regards the very concept of legal rights as an evil in themselves. Necessary in some cases perhaps, but evil. A legal process was and is something to be avoided at all costs. As a consequence of this philosophy China has little in the way of early written laws. What little written law exists stresses obligations and omits any mention of rights as they are known in the West. No civil law seems to have developed, and the early law centers on criminal matters. In 536 B.C. a book of punishments appropriate for various sorts of crimes was published. The list, which included castration and amputation of the feet, appears to have been written for its crime deterrence value.

In 350 B.C. an emperor published a criminal code applicable to his part of China. China was not united until 221 B.C. when Emperor Chin defeated all the other kingdoms and united China as one nation. About A.D. 50 the united Chinese empire established a criminal code for the whole of China, standardizing law and procedure for the first time. This code applied only to criminal matters however, and commercial relations remained unregulated by any legal system unless the matter rose to the level of a crime. Law in China continued to develop only in the area of criminal law. Interestingly, in A.D. 700 the Chinese developed the technique of fingerprinting to identify individuals.

This neglect of civil law is not surprising considering that Chinese thought, influenced by Confucius, suggests that a society should promote harmony among its members, and all policies should be measured against a "promotion of harmony" test.

The logic to this philosophy is evident when one takes into account living conditions in China. Life in a crowded place like China requires constant interaction with one's fellow citizens in an infinite variety of ways. These relations are too complex for the law to define the correct path in all possible situations, so any law will sometimes be applied in situations where it does not fit with unintended consequences, making some degree of injustice inevitable.

The Chinese philosophy about law is as follows: If a large body of law exists, people could study it and discover that they have legal rights. That knowledge is considered dangerous according to Confucian philosophy because the individual may seek to rely on legal rights rather than seek goodwill and work a compromise when a dispute arises. The specter of individuals noisily asserting rights is considered socially undesirable and certainly unharmonious. Rather than worry about rights, Confucian philosophy suggests that the individual should be concentrating on personal duties and obligations to society that are embodied in traditions, customs, and the teachings of Confucius.

If a harmonious society is the ultimate goal, imagine the damage done if an individual actually demands a trial. The image of two neighbors arguing vehemently in court about the boundary between their houses, with residual bad feelings that could last for years, is an image totally incompatible with the search for harmony. This scenario is considered a disaster regardless of who wins. In order to avoid this disharmony, all social groups should offer services to mediate the dispute peacefully. The parties should reach a compromise that preserves the dignity of all parties so that harmony and goodwill can once again be established between them. The needs of the community for peace and harmony transcend any entitlement on the part of an individual to insist on exactly what the individual is owed and all should be willing to compromise in a way that avoids embarrassment (loss of face) to the other parties.

So how does law fit into a community with such attitudes? It does not fit very well, and where law is used at all it is used differently from in the West. Because the purpose of the law is considered to be the protection of social order, much Chinese business regulation does not define the relative rights as between individuals, but rather is designed to protect society from discord, with penalties similar to criminal law in the West.

When the purpose of the regulation is to strongly discourage disharmonious activity rather than to provide a remedy for individuals, it makes sense that the penalties in Chinese commercial law seem quite harsh by western standards. Of course they exist primarily for deterrence and are rarely applied. Rather, the law is usually used as a model to declare what is acceptable in order to encourage the parties to settle peacefully. If a dispute is not settled, the court is likely to hold both parties responsible for not settling their disputes on a friendly basis, and it is not unusual for the court to imprison both parties in a lawsuit.

So, if the law is considered to be the wrong path toward social order, what is the right path? For the answer, we look back to Confucius who taught that people should live in an ethical way according to rituals that reflect the popular feeling about morality. If individuals live honorably and leaders lead ethically laws would not be necessary. If the leader is not honorable, laws would not protect the people anyway. Therefore the proper way to regulate society is to instill a sense of duty, ethics, and honor in people so that they will do the right thing without the disharmonious intervention of a legal system. In addition to applying law, courts should encourage the people to follow the rituals and customs that had, over the years, proven to promote harmonious relations between citizens. Such was the prevailing view as China approached the twentieth century. Obviously if duty, honor, and ethics do not prevail among the Chinese leadership, and they often did not, China offered little protection to the relatively powerless.

As China began to do substantial business with the West at the end of the nineteenth century, a new problem presented itself. Foreign businesses were oblivious of Chinese ethics and customs. They wished to be protected in their transactions by legally enforceable contracts. China had no such law available but it was necessary to have something in the way of commercial law to show the foreigners; so China adopted some commercial law, borrowing heavily from the new German civil codes. Many aspects of Chinese law were codified in the 1920s and 1930s. Thus it would seem that China had been placed in the Romano-Germanic family of law. But a nation as large and populous as China does not change because five volumes of law are filed in a library in the capital. The new codes were applied when they seemed to do justice according to Confucian philosophy but were otherwise ignored.

Chinese law further evolved when the country embraced Marxism in 1949. In fact, China embraced Communist philosophy even more vehemently than the U.S.S.R., quickly abolishing private property and collectivizing agriculture. Briefly, the U.S.S.R. tried to convince China to adopt similar laws in order to unify the Communist world. China did not do so. Marxist principles of sacrifice for the common good were more compatible with traditional Confucian philosophy than European codes and the Chinese rejected western-style law as alien to both Communist and Confucian principles.

Law did not develop much in China from the time of the Communist takeover until the 1978 economic reforms. At that time, China backed away from Communist economic principles somewhat and began to seek a place in world commerce. The reforms resulted in great economic growth and increased interaction with foreign business interests. Once again China's legal system placed it out of synchronization with the rest of the commercial world to the detriment of China's development.

China needed a legal structure compatible with the expectations of foreign traders and investors. A major effort was made in that direction with the enactment by the legislature, called the National People's Congress, of the General Principles of Civil Law (GPCL) in 1986. These principles are the present foundation for all civil law in China. They are squarely in the Romano-Germanic family of legal systems. The GPCL is a set of general principles and provides that previous law, incompatible with it, is ineffective. Future regulations must also be compatible with the GPCL. The GPCL is only a set of general principles, and it does not specifically cover many types of legal disputes. In such cases the GPCL directs the court to make decisions in accordance with state policies. Obviously this directive gives little comfort to foreign business.

Within the framework of the GPCL China has adopted its contract regulations. In the 1980s many of the specific contract statutes now in force were enacted.

A separate and distinct body of law developed for foreign contracts and investment as opposed to the law for domestic transactions. As time progressed and interest in commercial relations with China rapidly grew, the Chinese deemed it desirable to standardize their contract law. A major reform of contract law was proposed in 1981—with a further revision promulgated in 1993—called the Uniform Contract Law (UCL), which is likely to be enacted soon. The UCL is to be applicable to all types of contract relations except technology transfers, which are governed by a separate Technology Contract Law, and contracts between individual Chinese citizens that are governed by the GPCL. Contracts for technology, which is imported from

outside China, must conform to an act called Regulations on the Administration of Technology Import Contracts. In addition to being regulated by
the GPCL and soon the UCL, contracts of foreign business interests fall
under the Foreign Economic Contract law (FECL) passed in 1985.

Although China appears on the surface to have a well-developed contract law, Confucian principles permeate the new statutes and their application can still be arbitrary and vague. All contracts in China are subject
to the requirement that they be based on "equality and mutual benefit." Another requirement is that any contract not damage "public interests." A
court may void a contract if it is "unfair." If no specified performance time
is set in the contract, the court will not presume that each party must perform within a reasonable time as is common in the West. Each party may
perform its obligations on its own schedule. If the contract does have a specified performance date, the contract may not be enforceable in court. If a
seller fails to perform a sales contract within the specified time, some legal
thought presumes that the seller must be provided an extension.

These provisions give a judge great latitude to void or limit a contract
that an influential party wishes to back out of, and the accusation of bias
in Chinese courts has been commonly made. A frequent accusation made
by foreigners doing business in China is that a Chinese firm obtains an
American partner and learns the business, operating on the foreign capital
until the business becomes profitable. The Chinese partner then labels the
partnership contract "unfair." The Chinese firm next files suit in a friendly
court to squeeze the foreign partner out. If done with the cooperation of
local officials and the prior tacit agreement of the local judge, no practical
defense is available to the American partner for such a legalized swindle.

In addition to problems with the legal system, foreign business interests
in China complain that corruption among government officials, long a
problem, has worsened since the economy has been liberalized. The legal
system seems powerless to clean up the pervasive corruption in the government despite a few well-publicized executions.

Chinese contract law requires contractual intent similar to that in western legal codes, and most serious commercial contracts in China are required to be in writing to be enforceable. Assignments of contract rights to
others are not generally permitted without the consent of every original party
to the contract.

The remedies for breach of contract in China are generally either to re-
store the parties to the position they were in before the contract was made
or to order the parties to perform their contracts as agreed. Monetary damages, the most common remedy in the West, are less used in China even
though the GPCL provides for them.

In keeping with Confucian principles, Chinese law does not usually afford the parties a remedy in courts until they have attempted to settle their
dispute by mediation. If mediation fails to resolve the problem, the parties

must attempt to arbitrate the dispute, and only if mediation fails may they bring the matter to the "People's Court" to litigate.

In addition to contracts, the Chinese have modified their law in recent years to regulate investments in telecommunications, employment of foreigners, foreign trade, taxes, and tariffs. Prior to liberalization all business was state owned and no bankruptcy law was necessary. Today the adoption of new bankruptcy procedures seems to be a priority of China's legal system. Many of these changes are a result of China's desire to participate in the World Trade Organization.

One difficult issue looming between China and the West is the pervasive problem of the Chinese manufacturing of counterfeit copies of branded products. This problem was not serious in times past because, although counterfeiting was common, the quality of Chinese manufactured products was low, which made them readily distinguishable from the genuine branded product produced in the West. Since the 1978 economic reform process the Chinese have learned much about western manufacturing technology. Now many knockoff Chinese products are nearly indistinguishable from the genuine products, leading the brands' owners to complain loudly enough to be heard by their nation's politicians. This issue has adversely affected China in trade negotiations.

Despite the liberalization of China's economy, the Chinese government does not believe in, or practice, anything like western free market competition. Foreign investments must undergo a multitier screening process and are subject to many requirements. For example, many foreign-owned manufacturing operations are being required to export a certain percentage of their output.

China still attempts to control expatriation of its currency through a system of foreign exchange controls. However, small businesses, which simply ignore much government regulation, seem to be flourishing in China. The entrepreneurial spirit is alive in China, and many Chinese would rather own their small business than be employed by a bigger enterprise. This sentiment is characterized by the prevailing expression that "it is better to be the head of a rooster than the tail of a bull," meaning that it is better to own a small business than be a manager of a larger one.

Clearly, China's fledgling legal system, while adequate when China was an island unto itself, is insufficient to sustain long-term growth in the globalized economy. In fact, China has a legal climate that makes it a difficult and hostile place for foreigners to do business. The protections most large nations afford to foreigners are not available there. Improvements are coming but they are coming slowly, and it all takes place in an atmosphere of sometimes militant hostility towards nations that were formerly China's colonial masters. For now, caution is the keyword.

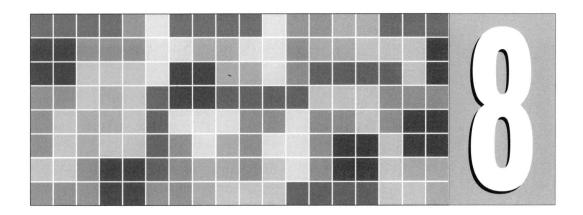

A Tour of the Law of Japan

relationship/mutual

Estern Oriental

The Western world experienced a period when it was united under the Romans, declined into feudalism, and then experienced a renaissance in which rapid development took place. Each period had a profound effect on the laws of Europe. Although certainly not parallel in many respects, Japan passed also through periods of unity, feudalism, and restructuring, and, as in the West, each period left its mark on the law.

The first period we shall consider is from the eighth to twelfth centuries. Japan entered this period heavily influenced by China, and Japanese societal structure developed roots in Confucianism. During the later part of the epoch, known as the Fujiware period, Japan moved away from Chinese influence, but Confucian thinking, with its emphasis on harmony and abhorrence of strict legalism, left an indelible imprint on Japanese society.

In 1280 Japan successfully repelled a massive invasion by the Monguls thanks in part to the intervention of a typhoon that wrecked most of the invader's fleet. Thinking their Shinto gods had acted to save Japan, the Japanese named the storm Kamikaze or divine wind. No other serious invasion attempt of the Japanese Islands was contemplated until 1945, but the events of 1280 were burned into the Japanese national consciousness. This supposed divine intervention made it difficult for Japanese to believe that they could ever be on the losing side of a military action that could cost them their sovereignty, even when they faced superior forces. Perhaps such thinking enboldened Japan to make a serious military blunder in 1941, as we shall explore later in this chapter.

As in China, the concept of personal rights does not manifest itself in early Japanese society, and little resembling western law can be found at all in Japanese history. The earliest semblance of law appeared around A.D. 650 in the form of *ritsu*, a list of things people were prohibited from doing. Another list of regulations for administration was called *ryo*.

To be blunt, early Japanese law is hard to find. The next stop in the search for it takes place in the twelfth century. Japan was then in a state of feudalism. The military class, or samurai, adopted a code of conduct for their members called the *buke-ho*. As is so with the *ritsu*, the *buke-ho* utters not a word about rights or morality. Rather, it is about the absolute duty of a military inferior to be faithful to those above his rank. The relationship is entirely one way. The soldier owes every duty and sacrifice to a superior, and the superior owes nothing at all to the soldier. The concept that anyone owed any duty whatsoever to one's inferiors, outside or inside the military, was alien to Japanese thought and some aspects of this viewpoint remain in Japan today.

Japan continued to develop rules and customs governing relations between those of equal classes such as warriors, merchants, or peasants. These classes were socially separated in Japanese daily life. No rights or protections were afforded those below one's class in society, and no rights or protections were afforded one from the whims of those above. As between members of the same class, a whole system of rules, called *giri*, developed to govern relations.

A *giri* covered nearly every type of relationship between social equals. For example, a giri dictated relations between father and son, landlord and tenant, merchant and customer, and so on. The giri was only a set of courtesies and not law enforceable by any sort of court. However, giri was strictly followed. To be perceived as one who failed to respect the giri would result in extreme embarrassment. So, although seemingly only a code of honor, giri was observed as carefully as laws were followed in the West. From the seventh to the twelfth centuries, Japan was united and cohesive with society strictly regulated by the giri. Law as it was known in the West within such a society did not exist and seemed unnecessary.

In the twelfth century Japan's warrior classes replaced the previous civil administrators with Shogun nobility and Japan entered its feudal era. The last of the Shoguns, the Tokugawa Shogunate began about 1600. Under the Tokugawa Shogunate, Japan adopted a policy of nearly total isolation from the rest of the world. Under this policy Japan did not trade or have much other contact with the outside world, and so Japan avoided any need to adjust the legal climate to accommodate foreign trade or business.

Japan's era of Tokugawa rule continued about 250 years, during which the rest of the world made considerable technical progress while Japan stagnated. A wake-up call came to Japan in 1853 when U.S. Navy ships sailed into Tokyo harbor demanding a privilege for American business to trade with Japan. The Japanese discovered that they were powerless to stand up to a modern navy and did not immediately resist.

By 1858 Japan had submitted to treaties forced on it by the United States, United Kingdom, Russia, France, and Holland. Like it or not, and they didn't, Japan was now in the stream of world commerce.

The imposition by force of commercial treaties caused considerable consternation in Japan. The Japanese concluded that if they couldn't keep the outside world out, perhaps they could control it a bit. Japan united again, and restored an imperial government in a new era called the Meiji restoration.

Under the new emperors, Japan embarked on a program of modernization, nationalism, and militarism. Although Japan modernized its technology and other aspects of its society, the concept of absolute loyalty to superiors survived the modernization in the old form. The Shinto religion widely practiced in Japan taught that the emperor was the direct descendant of the Sun god and was a deity himself. Therefore, to defy him was to defy a god's will and so the flow of power down, but not up, was reinforced.

In a remarkable feat of rapid development, Japan developed its technology so quickly during the Meiji restoration that when war broke out with Russia in 1904 the Japanese surprised the world by winning a decisive victory. In about 50 years Japan had advanced from its Dark Age to become a world power. With the success against Russia, Japan developed a new confidence that would eventually lead to dreams of a great Japanese empire throughout the Pacific.

Japan abandoned its former isolationism with a vengeance. The nation flexed its new muscles by establishing colonies in Taiwan and Korea. By the 1930s Japan was confident enough to begin a challenge to the United States and Great Britain for dominance in the West Pacific. In 1937 Japan was at war with China, which eventually expanded to include the United States as an enemy in 1941. Powerful in its own backyard, Japan could not match the industry, technology, and leadership of the United States. The sun set on Japan in 1945. The island nation was soundly defeated, humiliated, and occupied for the first time in its history. Once again Japan changed directions as will be discussed later.

All of these events had profound effects on Japan's formal legal system, but as with China, the legal system is not in the driver's seat of Japanese society. The basic regulation of internal Japanese society still results from the application of *giri.*

This history sounds a bit like the situation in China, but unlike China, Japan does have a well-developed formal legal system. During the Meiji era, modernization of the law was pursued as vigorously as the modernization of technology. Japanese scholars studied the legal systems of the world to determine what might be best for adoption in Japan. Common law was rejected as too cumbersome to develop in a country with no prior tradition of using it. French criminal law seemed quite good to Japanese scholars. Japan adopted a system of criminal law and criminal procedure based on the French codes in 1882.

In the area of civil affairs, the modernization of Japan was directed from the top down. Any new civil law had to be compatible with that mode of development. The German approach to law and society were considered relatively respectful of authority for a European country, and so its legal infrastructure was attractive to Japan. A Japanese civil code, which appears to greatly resemble the German civil code of the time, was enacted in 1898.

The next year, in 1899, Japan adopted a commercial code similar to the German one. In the same year Japan adopted its first national constitution. This adoption of western legal philosophy was so radical in Japan that a number of new words had to be added to the Japanese language in order to accommodate it. Formally, Japan's new law fell squarely in the Romano-Germanic tradition.

Although Japan now had law, that law was not much favored by the people. In a society that practiced blind obedience to the leadership, the law was seen as just a mechanism for the government to punish its enemies. For Japanese citizens, the law seemed to be a new form of giri, and to be brought into the legal system for any reason was a loss of face. Therefore the number of plaintiffs who were asserting their new rights in the courts were few. The spirit of Confucius was, and is, still very much alive in Japan.

Further radical changes took place in Japanese law after the 1945 defeat. In 1946 Japan adopted a new constitution, which, although imposed on them by the occupying Americans, reshaped Japan as a constitutional democracy. The constitution reduced the emperor to symbolic status, renounced war, and established the right to make law in a bicameral parliament called the Diet. It also formed a Supreme Court.

The constitution set up a democratic republic and gave the Japanese people roughly the same rights as granted in the U.S. Constitution, including the right to choose public officials by election. In one area it goes further than the present U.S. Constitution, because it contains a specific clause giving equal rights to women. For most Japanese families and companies, the giri still influences the role of women and the constitution takes the back seat.

This combination of eastern philosophy, Anglo-American-style constitutional government, and Romanist statutes, gives Japan and Japanese law its present flavor. Japanese law does not really fit the Japanese people, and Japanese people don't really like law anyway, but the people are changing and so is the law.

In recent years Japan has developed into a major trading power necessitating further contact with the West. Business contact with the West means cultural contact as well. Japan recognizes the need to have business practices and laws in synchronization with the rest of the world. Consequently Japanese business law is evolving rapidly and Japanese business-people are getting used to the idea of following it.

The foreigner wishing to do business in Japan may consult the Japanese External Trade Organization regarding the laws applicable to that specific type of business. Japan's Foreign Exchange and Foreign Trade Control Law regulates importing and exporting activities within Japan. It was adopted in 1980. It covers foreign payments, customs and tariffs, and issues regarding establishment of offices and acquisition of assets in Japan by nonresidents.

The Commercial Code sets out the requirements for foreign companies that wish to do business in Japan. They are not too complicated, but non-compliance can result in stiff fines. Three legal structures for foreign business are set out. The first is Goshi Kaisha, a form of limited partnership. Second is Gomei Kaisha, a form of unlimited partnership. The last is Kabushiki Kaisha, which is a type of corporation. All foreign business, regardless of structure, is required to appoint a legal representative in Japan and open an office in the country. Registration with the government is also required, and the public must be informed in a formal way that the company is conducting business in Japan.

Because Japanese business frequently had dealings with foreigners, the Japanese have addressed the problem of whose law should apply when a contract is made with a foreigner. The Act Concerning the Application of Law, or Horei, applies to transactions between a Japanese and non-Japanese and determines which party's nation's rules will apply in a contract dispute. However, no guarantee says that the Horei will agree with the rules in the nation of the other party, and these conflicts make for messy and expensive litigation. As a safeguard, any international business contract itself should specify the law that will apply to the contract in event of breach so that such conflicts may be avoided.

In the past Japan was not known as a place where intellectual property rights were carefully respected, which was a point of friction between Japan and its trading partners. Japan has addressed the problem with patent and copyright legislation. The patent law differs from most in that protection begins only from the granting of the patent, not from the time of the application. Protection lasts 20 years, which is the same period as in most of the world.

Copyrightable materials include literature, scientific, artistic, musical, dance, and theater works. Also included are architecture, films, photos, computer programs, and databases. Protection usually lasts for the author's lifetime plus 50 years. For movies, photos, organizational publications, and works published under a pen name, the protection begins at the time of publication and lasts 50 years.

Prior to 1994 Japan did not have a strict liability law for products, and it was necessary to prove negligence in manufacturing in order to sue a manufacturer for injuries caused by defective products. This burden was a difficult one to place on a plaintiff. Few suits were filed, and fewer still were successful. In 1994 law changes the burden so that the plaintiff only has to prove that the product is defective or, in other words, unreasonably dangerous, in order to collect actual damages from a manufacturer. Punitive damages are still not allowed. Even though these changes have not led to a flood of litigation in Japan, good engineering, warning labels, and product liability insurance are probably desirable for those exporting to Japan today.

Although they are not as important a part of the business climate as in the West, Japan's laws are better developed than in many other parts of the Far East and are a factor in doing business there. Fortunately, Japan is a unitary state and its laws are about the same all through the country. Japan does have 47 provinces called prefectures, but these provinces do not have as much autonomy as the individual states have in the United States. Local regulations and laws, although they may exist in Japan, are not as prevalent as foreign businesses may be accustomed to seeing at home.

The Japanese court system is a single national one. It is headed by a 15-member supreme court, under which are 15 appeals courts and 50 trial courts. Additional specialty courts handle routine legal matters, such as divorces. A single judge usually decides both the facts and the law in trials. Reversals on appeal are relatively rare. Japan has no right to a jury in a trial case. Judgments seem to be quite summary. Of all criminal cases filed, the result is a 99 percent conviction rate.

The future of Japanese law depends on the future of democratic thought in Japan. At present, Japanese law remains a work in progress and a fascinating blend of East and West.

Section II

An Excursion to the World
of Economic Integration

In many areas of the world, sovereign nations are no longer the top tier of government. In pursuit of economic advantages, nations are banding together in increasing numbers to reduce the barriers that impede business activities between them. These efforts take various forms depending on the depth of economic integration desired by the partner countries. Some regions prefer to make simple agreements, reducing tariff barriers but generally maintaining the sovereignty of the members in other areas. Individual members in other regions actually sacrifice many of their sovereign powers in order to form a fully integrated area. In such regions the trade bloc takes the place of national government in many important areas of governance. Let's take a look at the different types of trade blocs in the world.

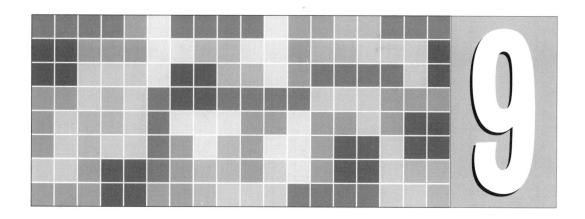

A Side Trip Through the Treaties of Regional Integration

GENERAL TRADE TREATIES (TRADE PROTOCOLS)

Many trade agreements do not purport to set up a trade bloc. These agreements are simply negotiated remedies to specific problems that occur between trading partners. Such agreements do not significantly advance the cause of economic integration. Rather they reduce conflict and uncertainty in trade relations as well as balance issues of protectionism. The most influential general trade treaty in the world is the World Trade Organization, which will be discussed in a subsequent chapter.

THE FREE TRADE AREA

The most basic form of economic integration is the free trade area (FTA). Nations that combine to form a true free trade area agree to allow other members' goods and services to flow freely over borders within the FTA. The agreement generally has little effect on goods from outside the FTA. Each member maintains its own customs service and tariff schedule for goods coming in from outside the FTA. Good and services from outside the FTA must pay duties to (and according to the regulations of) the nation the goods are entering.

If the goods are reexported from one FTA member to another FTA member, they must pay duties again to the country they are now entering. An FTA confers little advantage other than reduced tariffs, which are already often quite low between WTO members, and results in less overall economic integration than in other forms of trade blocs. FTAs are merely a beginning point for countries that wish to integrate further in the future, or a way to take present advantage of each other's economic efficiencies even though no expansion of the provisions of the FTA is contemplated.

THE CUSTOMS UNION

A customs union is similar to an FTA in that goods and services produced in member nations may move to other members relatively free of tariff and other barriers. In addition to this advantage, a customs union has a common customs scheme for the entire area. Goods entering a customs union from outside must pay any duty to the customs union in order to enter the territory of the trade bloc. The members, in a manner that they agree upon, share revenue from the customs union. Once within the customs union and the duty is paid, goods from outside may move freely within the customs union in the same manner as goods produced within the customs union. Neither customs unions nor free trade areas address any issues other than trade in goods and services. Customs unions and FTAs generally do not have agreements with regard to mobility of capital, labor, or other factors of production.

THE COMMON MARKET

A common market has the characteristics of a customs union with one great additional factor. The common market further integrates the economies of the member states by including significant agreements regarding the factors of production. Factors of production are ingredients, such as capital investment, labor, and technology, that make more efficient production of goods and services possible. Common market agreements frequently confer wide latitude for citizens of the member states to live and work within the national territory of the other members. The private companies or individuals of each member may make investments in other member nations. These labor, capital, and immigration agreements may exist in vestigial form in customs unions and free trade agreements, but a common market generally lifts nearly all restrictions on immigration and the mobility of labor and capital within the common market. Goods coming in from outside are treated in the same manner as in a customs union.

ECONOMIC UNION

An economic union is an attempt to break all national barriers to business activities between the member nations. Member nations essentially give up economic sovereignty to the economic union. After the economic union is formed, international business activities between the businesses of the members are similar in most respects to domestic activities. Goods and services as well as factors of production move freely within the area. In addition, the members attempt to standardize other national regulations affecting business activities, such as tax regulations, health and safety standards, and labor regulations, so that most barriers to international business between the members are removed.

POLITICAL UNION

The most comprehensive form of economic integration is the political union. At this point the national governments of the countries diminish greatly in importance as a supernational government created by the political union takes over or influences many traditional national government functions such as social policy, defense, general taxation, and so forth.

In a political union the members virtually cease to exist as sovereign nations and shift to become more of the nature of a province within the new supernation created by the political union. The European Union, since adoption of the Single European Act, is currently the only large political union.

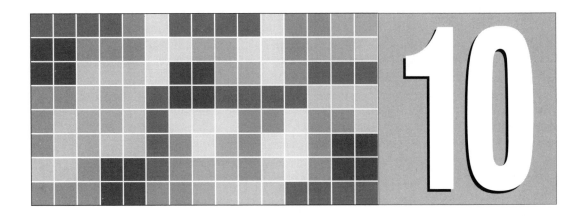

A Side Trip to MERCOSUR

At the same time that great attention has been given recently to the economic integration in North America and in Europe, a new and exciting agreement has been rapidly developing in South America. The Mercado Comun del Sur (Common Market of the South) is commonly known by its Spanish acronym, MERCOSUR.

MERCOSUR had its inception in the 1980s when Brazil and Argentina signed a number of trade protocols. In 1988 Brazil and Argentina set up a common market between the two countries, and in 1991 the Treaty of Asuncion was signed adding Paraguay and Uruguay as full members forming present-day MERCOSUR.

The total population of MERCOSUR is about 250 million. The land area, 12 million square kilometers, is about the same as the continent of Europe.

The biggest nation in MERCOSUR is Brazil. With a land area just smaller than that of the United States, Brazil is also the largest economy in Latin America. Brazil's GNP per capita of about $6,000 remains much lower than that of Argentina, but Brazil's total economy is much larger due to its size and population of nearly 200 million. This large and powerful nation has a diverse economy based on agriculture, mining, manufacturing, and services.

Argentina is the second-largest country in MERCOSUR and the second-largest country in South America (after Brazil) with a land area about 30 percent of the size of the United States. The population is just under 40 million. It is by far the richest member of MERCOSUR with per capita income above $10,000. Argentina has been experiencing rapid economic growth in recent years fueled by abundant natural resources, a relatively well-educated population, and a diverse industrial base.

Paraguay is a land-locked country between Brazil and Argentina. About the size of the state of California, Paraguay is small but still more than double the size of Uruguay. Paraguay is the poorest MERCOSUR member with per capita income at about $4,000. It has a population of between 5 and 6 million.

Uruguay has a better economy and is somewhat an international banking center. Uruguay has a relatively small, but also relatively prosperous population of about 3 million. GNP per capita is nearly $9,000.

A number of other countries have expressed interest in joining MERCOSUR, among them Bolivia, Chile, Venezuela, Colombia, and Peru.

As previously stated, MERCOSUR was formed in the decade of the 1990s by the Treaty of Asuncion. Although a period of trade liberalization lasted several years prior to the treaty, the common market was put into place at the end of 1994. This formative event occurred after the formation of the North American Free Trade Agreement (NAFTA). Nevertheless, MERCOSUR has already far surpassed NAFTA in the depth of integration of its four member nations.

MERCOSUR is an ambitious organization. It has already nearly eliminated tariffs between its members and has made good progress in lifting non-tariff barriers to trade. In the process of forming a customs union, MERCOSUR has established a common external tariff, but the plans for MERCOSUR go far beyond its trading relationships. MERCOSUR is beginning to coordinate the policies of its members in such widely diverse areas as agriculture, industry, monetary, transport, and communications. MERCOSUR is clearly on the road to becoming a common market, if not an economic union.

The structure of MERCOSUR is still in development. At present the highest authority in the organization is the Common Market Council. The Council consists of the foreign ministers and economic ministers of the member countries. They meet when they have business to conduct, but at least annually. Decisions are made by consensus.

Executive authority in MERCOSUR rests in the Common Market Group, overseen by the foreign ministers of the members who constitute the permanent representatives to the Common Market Group. In addition to the permanent representatives, each member state appoints an additional temporary representative to the Common Market Group. The Common Market Group enforces the terms of the MERCOSUR agreements and implements practical means of furthering the aims of the organization. This group meets four times each year, and decisions within the group are made by consensus.

MERCOSUR maintains an administrative office to handle the necessary documentation and translate all business back and forth between the official languages of MERCOSUR. They are, of course, Spanish and Portuguese.

A number of subgroups also work on proposals for consideration by the Common Market Council. These groups are composed of government representatives and members of the private sector. The groups are narrowly specialized in the following areas:

1. Commercial matters

2. Custom matters

3. Technical standards

4. Tax and monetary policies relating to trade

5. Land transport

6. Sea transport

7. Industrial and technology policies

8. Agricultural policy

9. Energy policy

10. Coordination of macroeconomic policies

11. Labor, employment and social security matters

MERCOSUR is organizing a parliament to legislate statutes affecting the entire region. A joint parliamentary committee exists to advise the council on how such a parliament should be formed and how national laws must be adjusted to harmonize with regional policies. Each member nation sends 16 delegates to the parliamentary committee for a term of at least two years. Decisions are made by a majority of the members.

Citizens of any MERCOSUR member are generally permitted to invest in the other members' countries in the same manner as the other nation's citizens. This national treatment covers investments in all types of assets including corporate shares, securities, intellectual property, and public incentives to investment, which are extended to nationals. Interestingly, the U.S. dollar is an official currency for such investments in additional to the four national currencies of the members.

If disputes arise between member nations of MERCOSUR, the members are encouraged to first negotiate directly with each other in an attempt to reach an amicable settlement. If no such settlement is achieved, any nation may request that the dispute be arbitrated. The arbitration will take place before an ad hoc court that will set up its own rules. Each state in MER-COSUR appoints 10 arbitrators, experienced in judicial matters, to an arbitration panel. Each of the two nations that is a party to the dispute chooses one from the panel to serve on each case. Those two choose the third panel member who then becomes the presiding judge. The decision is normally rendered within two months of the choice of the judges although a 30-day extension is permissible. Decision is by majority vote.

Any commercial dispute between private citizens of different MERCO-SUR countries is handled differently. Claims are filed before the Common Market Group representative of the country where the aggrieved party resides. If the aggrieved party's Common Market Group representative determines that the claim has merit it presents the claim to the Common Market group representative of the alleged offending country. The Common Market Group then appoints a panel of experts to make a recommendation whereupon the Common Market Group may or may not take corrective action.

One intriguing bit of evidence that MERCOSUR is serious about regional integration is an agreement that each will accept credit from the primary and secondary schools, as well as official institutions, of the other nations. This arrangement facilitates the transfer of workers and their families from nation to nation and makes it easier for workers to comply with licensing requirements in the other members' territories.

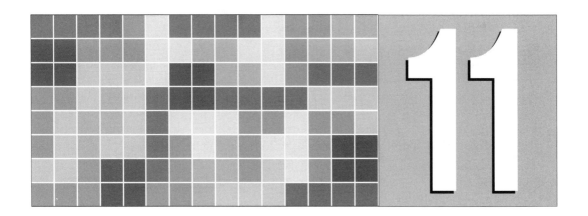

A Side Trip to Free Trade in North America (NAFTA)

big energy mkt

The North American Free Trade Agreement (NAFTA) is a little different from other trade agreements. The reason is the diverse nature of the partners. Each of the three members, Canada, Mexico, and the United States comes to the NAFTA table with different and complimentary capabilities, but each also has a different culture and perspective.

Canada has a small population of only about 31 million. Most, nearly 90 percent of its residents, are of European origin with the rest largely Asian. Canada has a huge land area, larger than that of the United States and, indeed, every other country on Earth except the Russian Republic. For comparison, Canada is about one-half the size of the continent of South America! It is blessed with tremendous natural resources.

In terms of annual national product, Canada is clearly second after the United States with about $22,800 (US$) per capita. Most of Canada's trade, about 80 percent of both exports and imports, is with the United States.

Canada exports little to Mexico and imports only a tiny percentage of its total imports from Mexico. With respect to Canada, Mexico's entry into NAFTA has not been significant.

Mexico has a much larger population than Canada, topping 100 million as of this writing. About 60 percent of Mexicans are an ethnic mixture of Native American and Spanish, with many of the remainder being Native American. About 10 percent of Mexicans are of European origin. Mexico's land area is about three times that of the state of Texas with a fertile plateau in the center and the rest of the land ranging from desert to jungle.

As with Canada, the United States is Mexico's dominant trading partner with the United States receiving nearly 90 percent of Mexico's exports. The United States sends Mexico the largest part of Mexico's imports as well. Mexico is not comfortable with this dependence and has addressed its discomfort in different ways. Mexico has negotiated trade agreements with other countries in Latin America and has made a free trade agreement with the European Union. Mexico sends a little more than 1 percent of its export products to Canada, which, despite the small number, is its second-largest export market after the United States. Imports from Canada are about 2 percent of Mexico's total, but these imports trail those from Japan and Germany in total amount. Of the NAFTA partners, Mexico, at about $8,000, is by far the poorest of the three NAFTA members in terms of per capital GDP.

How can one describe the United States in a few sentences? What should be mentioned and what should be omitted? The powerful $8.5 trillion economy? The advanced technology? The $31,000 GDP per capita? The population approaching 300 million? The abundant resources? The great diversity of its peoples? The United States cannot be described in a few sentences, and the attempt won't be made here. A description of the United States' relationship with its NAFTA partners is an easier task.

Canada comprises about 20 percent of both the U.S. imports and exports. Mexico accounts for about 10 percent of both.

NAFTA began with a free trade agreement that took effect in 1989 between the United States and Canada. Some mild discussion and criticism of the agreement in both countries, particularly in Canada, centered on the probability that Canada would be simply assimilated, economically speaking, by the United States.

The implementation of the U.S.–Canada FTA in 1989 was quite harmonious. Little economic impact was felt as all tariffs except a few on agricultural products had been eliminated the year before. The two nations already had low tariffs between each other for years, a long history of friendly relations, and relatively similar cultures. Although wage differentials existed, they were not too great, given that both nations were fully developed first world countries. Things were a little different as Mexico appeared on the horizon.

On the surface, Mexico would seem an unlikely free trade partner for both the United States and Canada. Canada had little economic relationship of any sort with Mexico before NAFTA, and relations between the United States and Mexico had not been nearly as harmonious as between the United States and Canada. Mexico had a history, with some justification, of fearing and resenting the "Colossus to the North" as one Mexican president described the United States.

Mexico's decision to enter into free trade with the United States and Canada was painful and contrary to its history. Mexico had treasured its culture and sovereignty. Mexican politicians had made a practice of blaming many of Mexico's internal troubles on the United States. By the end of the 1970s, however, Mexico was running out of choices. Mexican economic policies had been unsound since the 1960s. The policies were based on ever-increasing government intervention in private business, a policy of "import substitution" whereby tariffs were kept high to keep out foreign goods in an attempt to encourage development of industry in Mexico, onerous restrictions on foreign investment, and intellectual property laws that discouraged foreigners from introducing new technology into Mexico.

Despite these policies, which served to stifle economic activity, Mexico had passed a relatively prosperous period in the 1970s due to the discovery of huge oil deposits at a time when world prices were high. But Mexico's economy took an abrupt and catastrophic downturn at the end of the decade. As the administration of Mexican president Jose Lopez Portillo drew to a close, many had lost faith in the Mexican economy and capital was fleeing the country in huge amounts. Seeking help from the United States was difficult politically at that time, because Mexican politicians had made a habit of blaming their country's problems on the United States. National pride prevented the Mexican government from publicly advocating a bailout from the United States.

President Portillo responded to the crisis by nationalizing the banks and imposing currency exchange controls. Foreign investors were made apprehensive and because of this action further foreign investment in Mexico nearly halted. The next president, Miguel de la Madrid, was forced by Mexico's creditors and the International Monetary Fund to implement austerity measures. The result was a period that was painfully bleak for Mexican citizens as real wages dropped by half for ordinary workers.

The crisis continued throughout the 1980s. At the end of that decade, then-president Salinas de Gortari went to Europe to seek investment and trade agreements from the British or Germans. But Eastern Europe was in the process of throwing off communism and available Western European investment funds were targeted to that area. Margaret Thatcher of Britain bluntly told President Salinas that it was time for Mexico to get over its sovereignty complex and cooperate with the United States and Canada. She pointed out that former enemies in Europe, such as France and Germany, had put aside more severe past hostilities in the spirit of cooperation under the auspices of the coming European Union. The advice was taken under advisement and later was implemented.

But first President Salinas de Gortari initiated many major changes in the Mexican economy. He privatized many inefficient state-owned industries and closed others. Funds from the privatization sales were invested in public works for poor neighborhoods in a program called "Solidarity" ensuring broad political support. And at Salina's direction, Mexico changed its laws and policies to encourage foreign investment in Mexico.

Finally, President Salinas swallowed Mexico's pride and asked the United States for a free trade agreement. In June 1990, Presidents Salinas and Bush announced the negotiations would begin for a free trade agreement between the two countries. Shortly after, President Bush announced that these negotiations would be only the beginning of the trade initiative and that he would welcome a new trade arrangement for the entire hemisphere.

Canada then had a dilemma to resolve. Although it had little trade with Mexico, Canada was afraid that it would be left on the periphery of any other new agreements if it did not join the negotiations. Canada envisioned the United States attempting to set up a "hub and spoke" trading system where the United States would have separate trading agreements with its partners and therefore have special privileges with its partners that they did not have with each other. Investment would therefore flow to the United States because any goods produced in the United States could go duty-free to all the partners of the United States. So Canada decided it was in its best interest to have a trilateral agreement with future additions to join the arrangement rather than deal with the United States individually.

Canada also sought a more equalized approach to the Mexican market. Most Mexican goods entered Canada duty-free or with low tariffs even before NAFTA, but Canadian goods entering Mexico were charged tariffs of 15 to 20 percent. Canada made a request to join the free trade negotiations between the United States and Mexico in 1990 and negotiations began between all three parties the next year. By 1992, the basic agreement for NAFTA was reached and the three member nations signed it that December.

The text of the NAFTA agreement begins with the establishment of a free trade area with the objective of eliminating barriers to trade in goods and services. Also listed in the first chapter of the NAFTA as goals of the agreement are the promotion of fair competition, increasing investment opportunities, protection of intellectual property rights, and creation of a framework for further cooperation.

Chapter Three of the NAFTA treaty sets out the elimination schedule for tariffs. Duties on some goods were eliminated when the agreement came into effect in 1994. For the stated purpose of preventing too much economic disruption, tariffs on other goods were phased out after a 5-, 10-, or 15-year period. These phases have occurred or will occur in 1993 and 2003, with the last tariffs to be eliminated in 2008. Chapter Three also seeks to restrict some notorious nontariff barriers between the parties. Import licenses and quotas were phased out in most industries over a 10-year period. Export taxes were eliminated. Duty drawback programs, under which duties paid on goods coming from outside NAFTA were refunded if the goods were re-exported to another NAFTA country, are to be eliminated effective 2001.

This provision was of particular importance to the United States because of a Mexican program whereby components could be imported into Mexico, finished into goods, and reexported duty-free in 90 days or less. Had the United States not negotiated the end to such drawbacks Mexico might have been simply a way station for Asian manufacturers to add just enough Mexican value to qualify for NAFTA treatment and thereby export their Asian components to the United States nearly duty-free.

Prior to NAFTA, each future member had a unique and complex set of rules for the marking of goods. NAFTA standardized this "country of origin" marking. Finally, NAFTA eliminated any charges for using the services of a member's customs service.

The largest impact of these tariff reductions will be on the exportation of U.S. and Canadian goods to Mexico. Tariffs for goods entering the United States and Canada were previously quite low, usually only about 3 or 4 percent for Mexican goods, but the tariff on goods entering Mexico was relatively high, generally from 10 to 20 percent.

Although NAFTA is not a customs union, a common external tariff of just less than 4 percent was established for computer goods. Once computer goods have entered the NAFTA area and this duty paid to the member where they were originally imported, the computer goods may move to the territories of the other members duty-free.

Because most NAFTA goods presently do, or soon will, travel around the NAFTA area duty-free, it is important to understand the rules of origin, or, in other words, what is a NAFTA-originating good. Of course, goods wholly produced within the NAFTA area are certainly qualified for NAFTA tariff treatment. However, goods can, in other various ways, qualify for NAFTA tariff treatment with some facets of non-NAFTA components or labor. For example, if enough work is done on the goods to change their tariff classification into another classification of the harmonized tariff schedule, the goods will qualify as NAFTA products. Likewise if work done or components added within the NAFTA area account for 50 percent of the net cost of the good or 50 percent of the value of the finished good, the product is NAFTA qualified. The percentages change slightly for automobile-related goods. Textiles have their own rules whereby, regardless of value content, the yarn in any NAFTA-qualified textile product must be produced in the NAFTA area.

Chapter Five of NAFTA has to do with procedural aspects of collecting customs duties. Previously, each country had its own forms and requirements for a certificate presented with a customs entry spelling out the country of origin. Such country-of-origin certificates are now standardized with one form being used throughout the NAFTA area. NAFTA requires that shippers keep documentation to back up their claims of NAFTA origin for at least five years. If shippers are uncertain whether another member nation will afford their goods NAFTA treatment, they are entitled to ask their national customs service for an advance ruling that the goods qualify before shipping the goods.

Chapter Six of the NAFTA agreement deals with special issues regarding the energy sector. Mexico has constitutional and historical restrictions against foreign participation in its energy industries, and Mexico has reserved such activities to its government in the NAFTA treaty. In some cases, foreigners are allowed to participate in the Mexican energy industry, such as in electric power generation, but any electricity produced must be sold to the government electric monopoly. Petroleum production is still controlled by the Mexican government petroleum monopoly, but procurement for the energy industry is required to be opened over a 10-year period to other NAFTA members.

Shipments of less than $1,000 ($U.S.) value do not require a certificate of origin, but a member's customs service may require that a statement of the origin of the goods appear on the commercial invoice.

In Chapter Seven, NAFTA eliminates many tariff and nontariff barriers to agricultural trade and standardizes agricultural grading standards. It also requires trade barriers purportedly based on health or sanitary concerns be derived from sound scientific principles. In the past, all NAFTA members used unsound scientific pretexts. Such pretexts served as a guise for protectionism of local industries from imports. Export subsidies are prohibited except to counter subsidized imports from a non-NAFTA country.

Chapter Eight of the NAFTA treaty gives members a right to temporarily suspend tariff reductions or increase tariffs in order to protect industries that are inordinately hurt by the implementation of NAFTA. The key points follow:

1. It can be done only with the consent of the affected partner.

2. Action can be taken only on a one-time basis for any particular good and only for a maximum of three years.

3. The action must either be a suspension of duty reductions, or an increase in the duty rates. Any increase must be no greater than that charged for goods from nations having most favored nation status.

4. Compensation must be paid by the nation imposing the action in the form of trade concessions in other areas.

Chapter Nine of the NAFTA treaty addresses issues of technical standards for health, safety, environmental concerns, standardization, and so forth. Technical standards have often been used as nontariff barriers to imports, especially since the General Agreement on Trade and Tariffs and the World Trade Organization have largely eliminated protectionism through tariff schedules. The most important clause in Chapter Nine requires each country to notify the other prior to adopting new standards so that negotiations can take place.

Chapter Ten requires that various types of government procurement be opened to suppliers from the other NAFTA partners. The section only applies to federal procurement. State and provincial procurement are not addressed by NAFTA.

One of the most important parts of NAFTA, Chapter Eleven, protects investors of the member nations when investing in other member nations. The required treatment for such investors includes the following:

1. *National Treatment:* Each member must give foreign investors from other NAFTA members the same protections it gives its own nationals in a given situation.

2. *Most Favored Nation Treatment:* Each member must give foreign investors from other NAFTA members the same protections it gives non-NAFTA investors.

3. *Nondiscriminatory Treatment:* For any difference noted between national treatment and most favored nation treatment, the investor from the other NAFTA nation must receive the more favorable of the two.

4. *Minimum Standard Treatment:* NAFTA member investors should receive protection in accordance with international law.

Several previous practices, which had been required by Mexico, were outlawed by NAFTA. Among these practices were requirements that foreign investments export a certain proportion of their output, produce products with a certain level of content from the host country, hire senior managers within the host country, or have a certain number of citizens of the host country on the board of directors.

Mexico made a number of reservations to the foreign investment provisions. As to Mexico, these foreign investment provisions do not apply to a plethora of industries and activities such as the ownership of land near the border or seacoast, cable television, construction, automobiles, mining, transportation, and many others. The United States made a few reservations regarding these provisions, largely regarding safety issues in air transport.

Cross-border trade in services is addressed in Chapter Twelve of NAFTA. In the past Mexico has applied severe restrictions to non-Mexicans who wished to provide services in Mexico. The NAFTA treaty requires National and Most Favored Nation treatment for service providers from other NAFTA members. Citizenship requirements for licensing and certification of professional service providers has been eliminated. However, the licensing requirements remain the same so long as they are not burdensome to cross-border business and based on objective criteria.

Telecommunications were opened to competition from other NAFTA members by Chapter Thirteen both in the area of providing service and suppliers to the industry. This market had been severely restricted in Mexico.

Chapter Fourteen opened a small part of the Mexican banking industry to other members of NAFTA. Again Mexico had the severest restrictions in this regard, so the biggest changes take place in that country. Besides opening the banking industry to some competition from the other NAFTA members, Chapter Fourteen also opens the insurance, leasing, bonding, and foreign exchange services to citizens of other NAFTA members.

Chapter Sixteen provides some immigration provisions to help ensure that nationals of the members may have sufficient access to the national territory of the other members for business purposes to allow the effective implementation of NAFTA. The chapter provides for nationals of the member states to have temporary admission for business purposes, and entry for traders and investors, intracompany transfers, and it allows a limited number of professionals to travel and conduct business in the other members' countries.

Intellectual property had been a source of friction between the United States and Mexico for many years. Mexico's "industrial property laws" were onerous to foreign owners of copyrights, patents, and trademarks. The United States used the opportunity of the NAFTA treaty negotiations to seek more protection for intellectual property and Chapter Seventeen of the treaty does the job. It covers every type of intellectual property including copyrights on computer programs, films, sound recordings, as well as trademarks, patents, semiconductor circuits, industrial designs, and even trade secrets.

The remainder of the treaty has to do with administration, dispute settlement, and antidumping matters.

What has been the result of the NAFTA agreement since it was implemented? It is difficult to tell what changes in the U.S. economy were results of NAFTA and which would have occurred regardless. The first five years after NAFTA was implemented were some of the best in the economic history of the United States. Domestic product burgeoned from $7.1 trillion to $8.5 trillion. Employment increased from 109 to 127 million. Unemployment rates dropped from 7 percent to 4 percent. Inflation was low, and the national budget reverted to surplus. Between the United States and Mexico, two-way trade increased in virtually every sector. Mexican products that take advantage of the preference for NAFTA-produced fibers have, in many cases, replaced Asian textiles.

Between the United States and Canada, NAFTA made a less significant impact, perhaps because of the free trade agreement between the two nations before NAFTA. On the other hand, serious disputes have arisen between Canada and the United States in the areas of agriculture and publishing. NAFTA seems to be quite successful, but it is relatively new on the world stage and final results remain to be seen.

A Side Trip to Economic Integration in Western Europe

Where does one begin a discussion about Europe integration? The basic concept has been around a long time. The Romans succeeded in consolidating a large part of Europe, but that accomplishment hardly seems relevant to today's business. A Bohemian king proposed a European confederation during the Middle Ages. Victor Hugo envisioned a United States of Europe engaging in peaceful commerce with the United States of America in the nineteenth century. The motivation for action never materialized until the twentieth century, however, and it took some unique people to really make it happen.

Major changes in European thinking that led to the acceptance of integration only emerged after the two world wars. Before those wars, European countries were more concerned with their control over major markets and their empires. Many European powers had vast colonies outside of Europe, and so European powers focused on competition with other European countries in defending or acquiring colonies and capturing major markets for manufactured goods within and outside Europe.

Much of this conflict in Europe led to military action between European powers regarding issues of ownership and control over colonies. Through such conflicts Spain lost its empire long ago, and Germany was stripped of its empire after the First World War. The resulting national disgrace for Germany was a partial cause of the Second World War. After the Second World War, a great independence movement took place among former colonies around the world. Independence movements reverberated through many British colonies, such as India, where the British gave up the right to rule with a minimum of violence. The French attempted to hold onto their colonies a while longer, which resulted in violent but successful independence movements in Indochina and North Africa. Having lost in WWII, the Italians lost their colonial interests in North and East Africa. The Soviet Union used the occasion of World War II to build a new empire in East Europe, but this endeavor was also eventually doomed to fail with consequences that would be felt at the end of the twentieth century.

By the 1960s, the age of empires seemed to be over and competition between Western European powers for control of empires dwindled. Thus this empire building ceased to be a major source of friction between European nations in the decades after the world wars, smoothing the path for integration.

The other major source of friction between European countries was brutal economic competition between similar heavy industries located in different countries. This problem was serious. Its solution meant that traditional enemies would have to learn to work together. An exceptional person, Robert Schuman, would solve the problem.

Robert Schuman was a French statesman who had identity problems. He was born in Luxembourg, a decidedly German place. He lived in the Lorraine, and after the First World War when that area was ceded to France, Schuman became French. No sympathizer with the Nazis, he did not support the Nazi political agenda after the Germans occupied France in 1940. His disagreements with Hitler's philosophy earned him the honor of being arrested by Hitler's secret police, the Gestapo. After about two years he escaped from the Gestapo and participated in the French underground resistance until France was liberated in 1944.

As a hero of France, he entered politics after the war and held a number of important positions in the French government. But being German in a sense, he did not have the prevailing enmity for the new German government. He thought the two countries could work together now that Germany had embraced democratic ideals, and he considered the greatest part of the antipathy between the two countries to be competition between their respective coal and steel industries. Schuman set about devising a scheme whereby the two nations would peacefully divide this market between them.

The result was a new organization called the European Coal and Steel Community, designed from the ground up to avoid Franco-German conflict. Because Belgium, Italy, Luxembourg, and the Netherlands had been ravaged indirectly by the Franco-German conflict as well, they considered the goal of future cooperation between the former enemies to be a laudable one. Each joined the new consortium at its inception.

By 1954, most barriers to trade in the coal and steel industries were lifted between the members of the new community, and trade in these materials rose dramatically. The central authority fixed prices and production limits. The agreement worked quite smoothly over the ensuing years. The success of the coal and steel alliance proved the feasibility of future integration in Europe and further agreements were soon forthcoming.

By 1958 the coal and steel agreement had expanded and become the European Economic Community. Further agreement was made in the area of atomic energy. All three agencies, the Coal and Steel Alliance, the Economic Community, and the Atomic Energy Community joined as one in 1957 to become a six-member European community. At this point the present form of the structure of the European Union was formed. A council of ministers guided a commission as the executive branch, and a European Parliament legislated. The European Court of Justice was formed to handle judicial affairs of the new organization.

Britain petitioned to join in 1961. The United Kingdom's application to join was at first vetoed by Charles DeGaulle of France. Britain did join the Community in 1973 when DeGaulle was no longer a factor in the process. Greece came on board in 1981 followed by Portugal and Spain in 1986, and Finland, Austria, and Sweden in 1995. In a popular election, Norway rejected the opportunity to join.

The economic purpose of the European Community was to eliminate tariff and nontariff barriers between its members and make all of its members' territories a "single market." This goal was substantially achieved in 1992 with the completion of a customs union among all the members.

Several nonmembers of the European Union set up their own free trade area during this period. They were Austria, Norway, Sweden, Switzerland, Liechtenstein, Finland, and Iceland. This organization, called the European Free Trade Association, negotiated trade arrangements with the European Community, and several of its members ultimately joined the European Union.

The underlying basic purpose of the new European cooperation, to prevent a third European war, seems to have been realized. In the years following the Second World War, the centers of power in the world shifted away from Western Europe to the United States and the Soviet Union and Asia. The problems that have occurred in Europe and the European sphere of influence have indeed been dealt with cooperatively among the members of the European Community.

The European community has three treaties as its legal foundation:

I. The treaty establishing the European Coal and Steel Community (ECSC) was signed in Paris and entered into force on July 27, 1952.

II. The treaty establishing the European Community was signed in Rome and entered into force on January 1, 1958.

III. The treaty establishing the European Atomic Energy Community (EURATOM) was signed in Rome and entered into force on January 1, 1958.

Over the years the European Community has achieved "ever closer union," and in 1987 the European parliament adopted the *Single European Act* aimed at changing the membership into what is, for all practical purposes, one single nation. A treaty enacting the Single European Act was adopted at Maastricht in 1993, and the present day European Union supplanted the European Community in 1993.

The European Union today is the most closely integrated and developed supranational organization in the world. The individual members look increasingly like provinces in a huge European nation, and the institutions of the European Union look increasingly like a federal government. The total population of the European Union as of this writing was about 370 million in 15 countries although the EU is on the verge of expansion as it considers membership for some former communist countries. The present membership is listed here in the order that they joined.

1. Belgium

2. Germany

3. France

4. Italy

5. Luxembourg

6. The Netherlands

7. Denmark

8. Ireland

9. United Kingdom

10. Greece

11. Spain

12. Portugal

13. Austria

14. Finland

15. Sweden

The basic objectives of the EU include the following:

1. *To promote economic and social progress.* To this end, the single market was established in 1993, and the European Monetary Union resulting in a single currency was launched in 1999.

2. *To assert the identity of the European Union on the international scene.* This objective is met through European humanitarian aid to non-EU countries, common foreign and security policy, and common action in international crises. The members also attempt to take common positions within international organizations.

3. *To introduce European citizenship.* European citizenship does not yet replace national citizenship, but complements it, and confers a number of civil and political rights on European citizens. In keeping with this goal of European citizenship, a sort of European Union Bill of Rights has emerged that contains the following provisions:

   ■ Freedom of movement and residence throughout the Union.

   ■ The right to vote and stand as a candidate at municipal elections and in elections to the European Parliament in the state where the individual resides.

   ■ Protection by the diplomatic and consular authorities of any member state where the state of which the person is a national is not represented in a nonmember country.

   ■ The right to petition the European parliament and apply to the Ombudsman.

4. *To develop an area of freedom, security, and justice.* This objective articulates the basis for removing barriers in the operation of the internal market and the freedom of movement of Europe's people.

5. *To maintain, and build on, established EU law.* This objective includes all the legislation adopted by the European institutions, together with founding treaties.

THE EUROPEAN PARLIAMENT

In futherance of these aims, the European Union developed a number of institutions originally headed by appointees. These appointees were previously criticized for not being selected by a sufficiently democratic process.

Such criticism led to the establishment of the European parliament, which is the premier organization in the EU and whose members are directly elected by the people. As the EU's legislature, the European parliament does not directly originate legislation in most cases. Proposals are made by the Council of Ministers. Originally the parliament was merely a consultative body that gave advice to the ministers. However, later treaties have increased the role and influence of the parliament so that it now has some influence over EU legislation.

The Council of Ministers may no longer adopt legislation in some areas of governance such as environment, research, and economic development within and without Europe without first obtaining the opinion of the European parliament.

In the fields of labor migration within the EU, consumer protection, culture, health, and others, the parliament shares decision-making power with the Council of Ministers.

Agreements between the EU and other nations, acceptance of new members in the EU, and matters regarding the European Central Bank require the approval of the parliament.

In addition, the European parliament must approve the annual budget of the organization and provide oversight for the manner in which EU policies are implemented.

After each five-year period the European parliament appoints a new president and members of the European Commission. The parliament may force any of them to resign if they abuse their offices.

THE COUNCIL OF THE EUROPEAN UNION

Major EU legislation is considered and enacted by a council of the appropriate ministers from each of the member nations. Which ministers represent the countries in a particular case depend upon the subject of the legislation. For example, if the subject were regulation of working hours, the labor ministers would form the council. Final adoption of legislation is made jointly with parliament as already noted.

In addition to the legislative duties, this council coordinates the economic policies of the members. It also makes international agreements and prepares the budget, both of which require parliamentary approvals.

THE EUROPEAN COMMISSION

The 20 members of the European Commission head the executive branch of the European Union. The commission meets weekly to adopt proposals, submit policy papers, and otherwise coordinate the work of the Union.

The Commission first proposes the legislation of the European Union. If the Commission does not present a proposal the parliament cannot consider most types of legislation at all. The Commission is supposed to listen to all viewpoints and then propose legislation that is in the best interest of Europe as a whole. To this end the commission has a staff of about 16,000 employees and is the largest organization in the EU structure in terms of employment. Proposed legislation is screened by the principle of "subsidiarity," meaning that the European Union should legislate only in areas where it would be more effective than if the legislation were enacted nationally in the member states.

The European Commission enforces the treaties and legislation of the Union by referring breaching parties to the European Court of Justice or by taking other action. The Commission also manages the financial affairs of the EU, makes rules implementing legislation, and enforces the competition rules. Finally, it negotiates trade and cooperation agreements with nations and organizations outside the European Union.

THE EUROPEAN COURT OF JUSTICE AND THE COURT OF FIRST INSTANCE

The rule of law is upheld in the European Union by an independent judiciary composed of two courts. The courts hear cases in which the legislation of the European parliament is applied or in which the treaties that form the Union must be interpreted. Cases by private individuals and corporations against the EU's institutions are brought for initial determination to the Court of First Instance and appeals from those decisions go to the European Court of Justice. Other cases go directly to the European Court of Justice.

Both courts consist of 15 judges, appointed by the community as a whole for 6-year terms. The Court of Justice normally divides itself in three- or five-judge panels to hear cases, though at the request of a member state or at the will of the court, all 15 judges may hear a case together in a plenary session.

The Court of Justice hears two types of cases. A direct action, where an interpretation of EU law is needed, may be sent to the court from the Commission, other community institutions, or by a member state of the EU. The other type of case, a preliminary ruling, occurs when a court of a member state has a case before it that requires a ruling on EU law for resolution. Rather than guess at what the Court of Justice would do, the judge of a national court can present a question on EU law to the Court of Justice before making his or her decision.

Following its hearing, the court issues a written opinion that is translated into all official languages of the European Union and is available in bound volumes in a fashion similar to English case law.

THE EUROPEAN INVESTMENT BANK

The European Union is committed to help the poorer areas of its territory (called the "less favored regions") and improve EU infrastructure, particularly in the area of telecommunications, transport, and energy. It is also committed to protect the environment, improve urban life, and preserve the historic architecture of Europe. If a proposed project in one of these areas is deemed worthy and economically feasible, the European Investment Bank may fund it. The aim of the bank is to improve quality of life within the European Union, although the bank does finance some projects in less developed countries.

The European Union clearly seems to be the formation of a new nation from some of the world's older ones. This process has held great interest for observers who will undoubtedly enjoy observing the next big challenge of the EU, which is the accession of those nations that are the victims of now-discredited Marxism.

Section III
The Law of the Oceans and Airspace

Nothing is as basic to the understanding of the customs and treaties of international law as the age-old principles that guide the common use of the world's oceans and recent agreements about the use of the skies. A quick excursion through both subjects follows in this section.

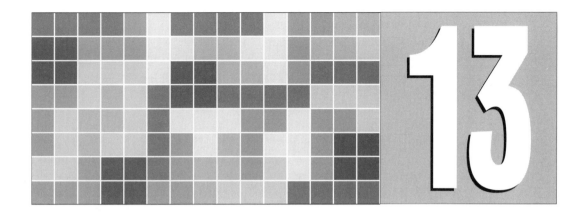

A Cruise Through the Law of the Sea

Is control of the oceans a topic to be addressed by legal scholars or by cannon fire and swordplay? Traditionally in history it was the latter, and from the harsh reality of military force comes our modern legal concept of a territorial sea and its contiguous zone.

From a naval perspective, having sovereignty over the shoreline gives a nation an opportunity to install a battery of naval artillery upon the coast. On solid land, it cannot be sunk. Such a battery has an obvious advantage over a battery aboard a ship that can be sunk. When artillery came into use, a nation could control that portion of the ocean where it could successfully fire a metal projectile through the hull of an intruder from its shoreline.

How much ocean could be controlled in this manner depended upon the range of the nation's best howitzer. In general, a large smoothbore cannon charged by a primitive propellant such as a saltpeter, sulphur, and charcoal mixture could, at best, throw a solid iron ball about three miles. Any ship that ventured within three miles of the coast could then be suddenly subject to the sovereignty of that coastal state. Beyond the range of the cannon, the sovereign had little power except what could be projected through its navy. The territorial sea, therefore, extended three miles from the shoreline in that era.

As the nineteenth century ended, human technology advances and great strides in naval artillery were made. Chemical propellants based on nitrocellulose appeared, which created much greater pressure in artillery tubes extending the range of artillery. Advances in metallurgy made it possible to manufacture guns capable of containing these greater forces without bursting. Meanwhile, artillery tubes were rifled causing the projectile to spin in flight greatly improving accuracy at long ranges.

As the twentieth century began, military control, using the new cannon, extended from the coastline to as far as 12 miles. Later in the twentieth century further advances in military technology resulted in aircraft and submarines. These developments made the use of coastal artillery less relevant from a military standpoint, but from a legal standpoint the need to define the territorial sea of a nation still remained.

THE TERRITORIAL SEA

The modern scheme to define a nation's territorial waters was developed by the United Nations treaty called the "United Nations Convention on the Law of the Sea," signed in Geneva in 1958. The treaty formally defines a belt of sea, adjacent to the coast, as the territorial sea of a nation. Sovereignty is expressly granted to a nation on, in the subsoil beneath, and in the airspace above its territorial sea.

In more recent years the 3-mile rule is falling by the wayside in favor of a 12-mile territorial sea. The 12-mile limit is permitted in a 1982 update to the 1958 treaty as follows:

> Every State has the right to establish the breadth of its territorial sea up to a limit not exceeding 12 nautical miles, measured from baselines determined in accordance with this convention.

The update clearly states that the territorial sea extends up to 12 nautical miles from the baseline, but to understand where this territorial sea ends one must first understand where to find the baselines. The treaty lays out a number of rules for this purpose. The most basic rule is as follows:

> Except where otherwise provided in this Convention, the normal baseline for measuring the breadth of the territorial sea is the low-water line along the coast as marked on large-scale charts officially recognized by the coastal State.

The low-water line is normally the average water's edge at low tide. Of course a nation's territory is at its largest, and therefore the baseline is extended into the sea the most, at low tide.

Defining the baseline is simple for a fairly regular coastline, but a "regular coastline" is often the exception rather than the rule. Many coastlines have deep indentations, barrier reefs, bays, and rivers running into them and so forth. The treaty resolves all such situations, as we shall see. What happens in the case of an island with a reef off the coast?

> In the case of islands situated on atolls or of islands having fringing reefs, the baseline for measuring the breadth of the territorial sea is the seaward low-water line of the reef, as shown by the appropriate symbol on charts officially recognized by the coastal State.

So we just go to the seaward side and find the low-water mark as before.

If the coast has deep indentations, such as a bay or fjord, a nation may draw a line across the mouth of the bay or fjord as long as it does not alter the general direction of the coast.

Some nations have overreached on this provision, notably the 1981 claim by Libya that it could draw a baseline across the entire Gulf of Sidra attempting to designate that entire section of the Mediterranean as Libya's territorial sea. Libya's leader Khadafi named this baseline the "Line of Death" for any unvisited visitors. The United States challenged that assertion by the deployment of its Mediterranean naval fleet to the area. Libya responded by sending two jets that fired upon aircraft launched from the USS *Nimitz*. When that fire was returned, both Libyan aircraft were destroyed, and it was the last the world heard of Libya's claim to an extension of the territorial sea.

The result was legally correct; the Gulf of Sidra is not a bay according to the definition in the treaty. A bay must enclose water and the Gulf of Sidra is a mere indentation in the coastline.

> For the purposes of this Convention, a bay is a well-marked indentation whose penetration is in such proportion to the width of its mouth as to contain land-locked waters and constitute more than a mere curvature of the coast. An indentation shall not, however, be regarded as a bay unless its area is as large as, or larger than, that of the semi-circle whose diameter is a line drawn across the mouth of that indentation.

A bay may only be completely closed off if its entrance is less than 24 miles. If it is greater, a nation may use a series of 24 miles of baselines in order to enclose the maximum possible area. It may not completely enclose the entire bay.

In areas such as river deltas, the coastline may be unstable, shifting about after storms or floods. In such cases the coastal nation may draw the baseline according to the rules cited in the treaty but need not move it landward if a subsequent change occurs in the coastline. Where a river flows into the sea the baseline may be drawn straight across the mouth of the river.

Where two coastlines are adjacent so that territorial seas would normally overlap, the territorial sea of each nation extends to half of the distance between the two baselines.

Where the coasts of two States are opposite or adjacent to each other, neither of the two States is entitled, failing agreement between them to the contrary, to extend its territorial sea beyond the median line every point of which is equidistant from the nearest points on the baselines from which the breadth of the territorial seas of each of the two States is measured. The above provision does not apply, however, where it is necessary by reason of historic title or other special circumstances to delimit the territorial seas of the two States in a way which is at variance therewith.

Any waters inside the baselines are internal waters of the nation and the nation has complete sovereignty over them.

As this book is written, China has claimed that 200 miles of the waters off their coast in the South China Sea is off limits to the U.S. Navy. The U.S. Navy ignored the claim and continued to fly reconnaissance flights over the area. U.S. and Chinese aircraft suffered a collision as a result of the Chinese attempts to enforce their claim. The Chinese airplane was lost and its pilot killed and the American crew captured and briefly detained. Certainly, the Chinese premise will not be accepted and the U.S. Navy will continue to assert its presence in order to reaffirm this important principle of international law.

RIGHTS OF NATIONS IN THEIR TERRITORIAL SEAS

The territorial sea is under the sovereignty of the coastal nation and that nation has the right and duty to govern it for the good of its people, commerce, and the environment. These privileges are granted to coastal states for governing their territorial seas:

(a) the safety of navigation and the regulation of maritime traffic;

(b) the protection of navigational aids and facilities and other facilities or installations;

(c) the protection of cables and pipelines;

(d) the conservation of the living resources of the sea;

(e) the prevention of infringement of the fisheries laws and regulations of the coastal State;

(f) the preservation of the environment of the coastal State and the prevention, reduction and control of pollution thereof;

(g) marine scientific research and hydrographic surveys;

(h) the prevention of infringement of the customs, fiscal, immigration or sanitary laws and regulations of the coastal State.

RULES FOR SHIPS IN THE TERRITORIAL SEA

Ships of all nations have a general right of innocent passage through the territorial seas of other nations. They should generally be permitted to pass through without interference unless special circumstances are present as described in the following paragraphs. Ships of noncoastal nations may also exercise this right. It is not permitted for a ship exercising the right of innocent passage to enter or intend to enter the internal waters of the state, or depart from the internal waters of the state. If it does so, the passage is not considered innocent and the ship is completely subjected to the authority of the state.

Traditionally a ship may not stop and anchor when exercising innocent passage but the most recent convention recognizes the right to stop and anchor as long as that activity is in the course of "ordinary navigation." Of course a ship may stop and anchor in times of distress or force majeure (i.e., great and unforeseen forces, such as hurricanes).

A passage that disturbs the peace of the state, such as a warship steaming by with guns trained on a village, is not considered innocent. Neither is the passage of a fishing vessel operating in contravention of the fishing laws of the state considered innocent. A submerged submarine is not innocent per se, and any submarine intending to exercise innocent passage is required to navigate on the surface and fly its national flag. Many activities considered inconsistent with innocent passage are delineated in the treaty:

(a) any threat or use of force against the sovereignty, territorial integrity or political independence of the coastal State, or in any other manner in violation of the principles of international law embodied in the Charter of the United Nations;

(b) any exercise or practice with weapons of any kind;

(c) any act aimed at collecting information to the prejudice of the defense or security of the coastal State;

(d) any act of propaganda aimed at affecting the defense or security of the coastal State;

(e) the launching, landing or taking on board of any aircraft;

(f) the launching, landing or taking on board of any military device;

(g) the loading or unloading of any commodity, currency or person contrary to the customs, fiscal, immigration or sanitary laws and regulations of the coastal State;

(h) any act of willful and serious pollution contrary to this Convention;

(i) any fishing activities;

(j) the carrying out of research or survey activities;

(k) any act aimed at interfering with any systems of communication or any other facilities or installations of the coastal State;

(l) any other activity not having a direct bearing on passage if the vessel is properly exercising its right of innocent passage, the nation owning the territorial sea may not interfere with it and is required to notify it of any known hazards to navigation.

If the passage is not innocent, such as a vessel involved in smuggling to the state, or if the vessel is proceeding to the internal waters of a state, that state has the right to prevent its passage or set conditions for its entry.

Although the right of innocent passage must generally be respected, a nation has the right, after prior publication, to suspend the right of innocent passage temporarily. If such a suspension is ordered, it may not discriminate between foreign ships. However, a strait used for international navigation may not be closed. Additionally, a nation may not charge for the right of innocent passage through its territorial sea unless the charges are specified services and apply to all ships without discrimination.

A nation may not board a ship exercising innocent passage in its territorial sea in order to arrest someone for a criminal act unless the act has consequences extending to the coastal nation, the arrest is made at the request of the captain, or the arrest is necessary for the suppression of narcotics traffic. Any other crime aboard a ship either exercising innocent passage, or on the high seas, is within the jurisdiction of the nation that registered the vessel.

Innocent passage is necessary for jurisdiction to pass to the flag of the vessel. An arrest by the coastal state can be made if the ship is leaving the internal waters of the state. If the ship is entering a nation's territorial sea from a voyage originating in another nation, and is merely using the territorial sea as a route to a third nation, no arrest can be made for a crime that was committed on the high seas or in the territorial sea and that does not directly affect the nation owning the territorial sea. Jurisdiction for such a crime lies in the state of the flag of the vessel. These same rules apply generally to civil matters as well as criminal ones.

THE CONTIGUOUS ZONE

Although the territorial sea may extend only 12 miles from the baseline, a coastal nation's jurisdiction is not always ended there. The coastal nation may still exert some control an additional 12 miles beyond the territorial sea under provisions of the treaty which provide for certain privileges in the contiguous zone. The rights of a nation within its contiguous zone are as follows:

(a) prevent infringement of its customs, fiscal, immigration or sanitary laws and regulations within its territory or territorial sea;

(b) punish infringement of the above laws and regulations committed within its territory or territorial sea.

By its definition the contiguous zone may not extend beyond 24 miles from the baseline.

CUSTOMS OF THE SEA THAT HAVE EVOLVED INTO LAW

Although much of the law regulating the use of the oceans has been adopted by seafaring nations as treaties, other aspects of the international law of the sea are in the form of long-standing customs. These customs may be recognized as the legal standard even though they have not been formally agreed upon as conventions. These customs have set standards that courts will often enforce, and so they take the character of law.

A lack of space in this book prevents a complete discussion of the customs of the sea, but an example is in order and the Birkenhead Drill is the best of them.

The *Birkenhead* was an English passenger ship that was caught in a terrible storm in the Indian Ocean in 1853. When it became obvious that the vessel would be lost, the captain determined that the ship should be abandoned. Unfortunately, as was common at the time, the *Birkenhead* did not carry a sufficient number of lifeboats to accommodate all aboard. The famous order issued by the captain, "Women and children first, men stand fast," was heeded by all. The women and children on board were saved while 445 men drowned.

The standard set by the captain of the *Birkenhead* is known as the "Birkenhead Drill," in honor of those who sacrificed themselves in the incident. It sets forth the priorities for saving life when such an unhappy choice must be made. Under the Birkenhead Drill, women and children should be the first to be saved, followed by the male passengers, followed by the ordinary seamen, and followed by the officers. The last to leave should be the captain of the vessel. The captain is not required to "go down with the ship" as is thought in popular folklore. Rather, he is required to remain aboard until all has been done that can be done to save others.

The Birkenhead Drill has been widely respected with a few infamous exceptions. One exception was the 1991 case of the *Oceanos*, a Greek cruise ship that floundered near the same spot where the *Birkenhead* sank. In the *Oceanos* case, the captain and many of the officers and crew disregarded the Birkenhead Drill. Most of them abandoned ship first, leaving 361 passengers aboard to take care of themselves. The captain and five of his officers were later convicted on criminal charges of dereliction of duty. The court applied the Birkenhead Drill as the standard of conduct.

As an aside, it is worth noting one of the heroes from this story. Actually, little is mentioned about her except what appeared in news accounts at the time. Her name is Lorraine Betts, and she is from Kenya. She was the cruise director of the *Oceanos*. Her job was to entertain the passengers, so technically she was an officer of the vessel and she rose to that responsibility. While the other crew fled in terror, she remained aboard the doomed *Oceanos* with her passengers and coordinated the rescue efforts. The vessel was lost, but all of the passengers were saved. Hats off to this officer who helped to preserve a fine tradition of the sea.

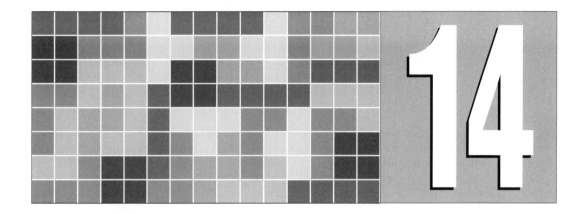

A Flight Through the Law of the Sky

Can the same principles we have learned regarding the use of the oceans also be applied to the skies above us? Being a newer technology than seafaring, aviation has no long tradition to rely upon and so it is governed more by treaty and less by tradition and custom than is ocean navigation. The basis of the scheme for the privilege to fly is found in a treaty signed in Chicago, known as the Chicago Convention on International Civil Aviation. It was signed during the last months of the Second World War in a meeting of the members of the International Civil Aviation Organization.

The treaty distinguishes between scheduled and nonscheduled flight. We shall first discuss the obligations of nations for nonscheduled (i.e., nonairline) flights. The treaty obligates each nation to extend to other members four general freedoms with respect to its airspace, subject to provisions discussed later. The freedoms are as follow:

1. Freedom to fly over the national territory and territorial sea of the other members without landing, similar to the right of innocent passage for ships in the territorial sea.

2. Freedom to land for nontraffic purposes such as to obtain fuel or repair a mechanical problem.

3. Freedom to discharge passengers, cargo, and mail that originated in the nation that registered the aircraft.

4. Freedom to load cargo, mail, and passengers destined to the nation that registered the aircraft.

5. The right to carry traffic between two foreign countries. (This fifth freedom has encountered resistance in many nations and has not been generally implemented.)

This treaty applies only to civilian aircraft and airports. It confers no rights upon military aircraft. Military airfields are not subject to the treaty unless they are also used for civilian purposes by scheduled international air services.

Generally, these freedoms apply to nonscheduled flight. Private or special-use aircraft may fly to or over any nation participating in the treaty, and nations are generally prohibited from requiring prior permission. Exceptions hold for safety reasons, such as terrain inaccessible to search-and-rescue efforts or where air navigation services are not available. In these cases a nation can require special permission for the flight or require the aircraft to follow approved routes.

With respect to scheduled flight (i.e., airline operations), the rules are a bit different. Scheduled flights require the expressed permission of the host country. Airlines may not operate in countries where they are not invited and, when allowed to operate, must adhere to the regulations promulgated by the host nation. The regulations must apply equally to domestic and foreign airlines. Nations are not permitted to have a separate set of regulations for foreign operators.

Most nations do not permit aircraft from another nation to operate for hire when the point of origin and the destination of the flight are both on its national territory. This design, known as a Cabotage law, is to preserve such activities for local providers and is permitted by the treaty. If the nation does give permission for a foreign air carrier to operate from point to point within the nation, it may not give exclusive privileges to only one other nation. It must allow others such privileges as well. Consequently, such domestic operations by foreigners are usually prohibited to everyone in order to avoid opening the door to the world.

Many nations have areas where military training takes place or research that is secret in nature is done. Other areas are not secret but are inherently dangerous to fly over, such as an artillery practice range or a nation's launch facility for its space program. Nations may legally restrict the flight of aircraft over such areas as long as the same restrictions apply to their own aircraft engaged in similar activities.

Scheduled or not, an aircraft entering the national territory of another nation may be required to land at an airport designated to be a customs airport for required processing by the customs and immigration services. If necessary, the aircraft may be searched and its documents inspected. If the host nation requires, such a visit to a designated customs airport may also be required upon departure. The list of designated customs airports must be published by each nation.

Each nation can make its own rules regarding the entry and clearance of customs and passport control, as well as quarantine of medical risks with respect to the passengers, crew, and cargo of an arriving aircraft. An exception is made for the aircraft itself and any spare parts and stores that are to be installed on the foreign aircraft. These items must be admitted duty-free if they depart with the aircraft. Civil aircraft may not enter a foreign nation with munitions aboard unless prior permission is obtained. Nations are obligated to take reasonable steps to prevent the spread of communicable diseases by air operations.

Nations are permitted to impose service charges upon visiting aircraft for using airports and facilities; however, such charges must be the same as the nation charges its domestic aircraft. Charges may not be made merely for the right of transit over the territory of a state.

Aircraft must have a nationality and be registered in only one nation. Each nation writes its own rules for the registry of aircraft and once registered each aircraft must prominently display its registration number. The list of registrations, including the names of owners of a nation's aircraft, must be made available to the other nations who are members of the International Civil Aviation Organization.

Nations must provide practical measures to help any aircraft in distress, including providing search aircraft when reasonable. In case of an accident, the state where the aircraft is registered may participate in the investigation and observe any inquiry.

Aircraft are required to carry certain documentation when flying internationally. As with an oceangoing ship, an aircraft engaged in an international flight is required to carry a manifest listing the passengers and cargo. Each nation is required to recognize the pilot's and crew's licenses if that nation has substantially the same requirements for license.

The law of the sky is still in development. More recent treaties involve remedies and extradition provisions to discourage hijackers and terrorists from using commercial aviation for their purposes. The sum of flying done in the world today is increasing rapidly and a number of new developments are expected to occur in the area of the regulation of international flying in the next few years.

Section IV

Clearing the Law of Customs and Immigration

Our tour of the world's law would not be complete without at least a quick look at the law of customs and immigration, the process by which people and goods are allowed to cross international borders. Because such law varies greatly from country to country, only a general overview is possible. The following is an explanation of those aspects that most nations have in common with respect to these subjects.

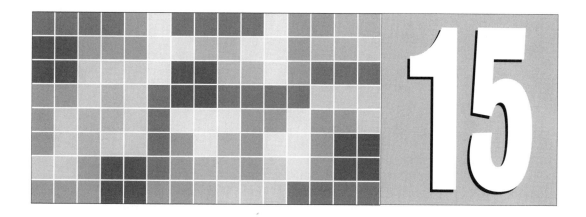

A Stroll Through Immigration Law

No traditional right to travel is recognized in the history of law. International as well as domestic travel has usually been a privilege afforded at the whim of the sovereign. The yearning for the liberty to wander the world is strong, however, and many great strides have taken place.

In 1215 the English, in search of greater freedom, revolted and through military action brought their King John to his knees. One of the freedoms demanded from the defeated king was the right to travel. The following was inserted in the Magna Carta, the document that began a process that ended the absolute power of English kings:

> All merchants may enter or leave England unharmed and without fear, and may stay or travel within it, by land or water, for purposes of trade, free from all illegal exactions, in accordance with ancient and lawful customs. This, however, does not apply in time of war to merchants from a country that is at war with us. Any such merchants found in our country at the outbreak of war shall be detained without injury to their persons or property, until we or our chief justice have discovered how our own merchants are being treated in the country at war with us. If our own merchants are safe they shall be safe too. In future it shall be lawful for any man to leave

and return to our kingdom unharmed and without fear, by land or water, preserving his allegiance to us, except in time of war, for some short period, for the common benefit of the realm. People that have been imprisoned or outlawed in accordance with the law of the land, people from a country that is at war with us, and merchants who shall be dealt with as stated above are excepted from this provision.

So as you see, the enlightened world began to recognize a right to travel, at least for commercial purposes. This concept has been steadily expanded in much of the world ever since.

Even though the right to leave one's country was becoming established, does one have the right to enter another? Generally, the answer is no. A sovereign nation may admit or exclude anyone it wishes, and that principle continues to this day. However, the new trade blocs such as NAFTA, the European Union, and MERCOSUR have agreements to require members to permit entry of citizens of the other members for limited commercial purposes. The European Union even allows the citizens of any member to be employed in the others without restraint of any kind.

In order to facilitate his subject's travel a king in times past might write a letter of introduction for his subject asking that foreign sovereigns extend that subject entry and any desired courtesy or privileges. One of the oldest surviving examples of such a letter is that of King Artaxerxes of ancient Persia around 450 B.C. It was written to those encountering his subject Nehemiah.

The letter was particularly addressed to the "rulers of the province beyond the river," and it requested that Nehemiah be given safe passage through the territory they controlled. Such letters were the forerunners of the modern passport, and the wording of a modern passport still sounds like a letter of introduction from the king.

By the time of King Louis XIV of France, such letters requesting safe passage on behalf of a subject became more common, and King Louis issued them routinely. Most long-distance travel at that time was by ship, and therefore the documents were used to enter and leave seaports. King Louis called such letters "passe port" giving rise to the modern English word *passport.*

A whole system of passport control was developed in Europe after that time and was widely used, but travel was not really common before the nineteenth century. As rail travel increased the numbers of the traveling public, the passport system was unable to cope with the volume. For a while, in the later nineteenth century passports were no longer used. They were revived in the twentieth century because of the need to control movement of people during the First World War. Passports have been in worldwide use ever since.

A number of international passport conferences were held between the world wars as the nations attempted to standardize their form, duration, and contents. The modern booklet form emerged from these conferences. Further agreements were made under the auspices of the United Nations in 1963, and new innovations, such as machine-readable numbers, continue to be introduced.

As stated earlier, each nation may set its own rules as to whom may be permitted entry to the national territory of that nation. A nation may refuse entry to any alien, set conditions upon which an alien may be allowed entry, or simply allow the entry. Many nations prohibit aliens from engaging in political activities, and most have special requirements for aliens who seek employment.

A nation may wish to screen aliens in advance and impose a requirement that a visa be obtained before the alien presents himself or herself at a port of entry. A nation may issue a number of different types of visas. For example, one type of visa might authorize employment, another permit multiple entries, and another permit crew of ships and aircraft the right to disembark while their conveyance is in port or on the ground. Another type of visa could confer diplomatic immunity or authorize participation in educational programs.

When an alien is admitted to the territory of a nation, it is customary to grant the alien the protection of that nation's laws in the same way that the nation protects its own citizens, particularly with regard to police protection from criminal acts.

Because immigration laws vary greatly from country to country, it is impossible to cover the details of any of them in a book such as this, but the information needed by a visiting businessperson is usually readily obtainable with a telephone call to the consulate or embassy of the country the person is contemplating visiting.

A Stroll Through Customs Law

Like the process of allowing the entry of people, the process of entering goods into a foreign country is formal and carefully regulated. Although the process varies from country to country, importing normally involves presentation of the goods for inspection along with the filing of various documents and payment of duties, if any.

Typically, importation of any form of goods requires an entry form summarizing the details of the transaction and stating the tariff classification of the goods to be imported. The tariff classification is important because tariff rates often vary according to the classification. Classification has traditionally been a difficult process because each nation promulgated its own rules but that process has changed in much of the world in recent years. The United States, Canada, and many other nations now use an internationally recognized and standardized system of classification called the Harmonized Commodity Description and Coding System.

Governments often require an invoice to accompany goods for importation. The invoice is normally provided by the seller and describes the transaction including the names of the parties, sales price, shipping method, and all costs associated with the shipment. If no invoice is available from the seller, such as when goods are purchased informally from a roadside merchant, the buyer may prepare a document similar to an invoice for purposes of clearing customs. Although not technically an invoice, such a document would include all of the information normally found on an invoice such as the sales price, delivery terms, and so forth, so that the customs service would have a written representation of the terms of the sale. This sort of document is known as a pro forma invoice.

Depending on the type of goods and the country, any number of other documents may be required, such as an inspection certificate that the goods comply with health and safety standards of the entering nation, a special invoice obtained at a consulate, a packing list, or perhaps an import license.

Nations often have different tariff rates according to the place where the goods or their components are manufactured or assembled. These distinctions are known as the rules of origin and can be quite complex. If the nation is part of a trading bloc, such as NAFTA or the European Union, the bloc rather than the individual country may determine the rules of origin.

Customs law is often quite complex, and specialists, known as customs brokers, are available to help one negotiate the process. Such a broker should certainly be consulted before any valuable property is shipped.

Section V

The Regulation of Advertising Around the World

Advertising plays an indispensable role in private business. It provides information, stimulates demand, enhances competition, and helps create jobs. Recent changes in the world's economy magnify the role of advertising as the need to spread commercial messages where they were hitherto unheard has increased meteorically. The phenomenon of globalization has resulted in the marketing in foreign lands of many products that in previous times were sold only in nations where they were produced.

It is usually necessary, when introducing a new product or service, to advise the local populace of its virtues through advertising. When confronted with this situation, the initial approach of many vendors has been to simply adapt their current advertising, which worked at home, to the new market. This adaptation was often done by merely translating the advertisement's text without consideration of any legal or cultural differences between the home and target countries. As a result, a morass of problems as a maze of laws, regulations, subtleties of languages, religious sensitivities, and other conflicts frequently assaulted marketers.

The lesson was quickly learned that the art of international advertising requires more than simply translating one's domestic campaign to the language of the new market. This section will present an overview of the environment for advertisers in various parts of the world, covering some aspects of culture and religion but concentrating, where they are dominant, on legal considerations.

A Jaunt Around the Law of Advertising in North America

The United States is clearly the world's leader for marketing and advertising. Modern advertising was developed there, and most of the world's biggest advertising firms are based there. The United States spends proportionately more of its national product on advertising than any other nation in the world.

Although numerous restrictive advertising regulations exist in the United States, they are not unduly onerous, partly because of the guarantee in the U.S. Constitution that speech and communication are protected. Although this provision was originally not applied to commercial speech, it has been extended to informational advertising by a landmark 1976 Supreme Court decision.

The courts have protected only the harmless dissemination of truthful commercial information. Any advertising propagating false or dangerous information can, and often is, severely restricted with the blessing of the constitutional courts. Numerous federal and state governmental agencies are involved in such regulation.

The flagship agency for regulating advertising in the United States is the Federal Trade Commission (FTC), which was established to guard against "unfair methods of competition in commerce." The FTC has a legal mandate to prohibit advertising that is false, deceptive, or unfair, and it has adopted regulations to that end. We shall examine these prohibitions individually to understand what the FTC forbids.

1. *False advertising* is advertising that is misleading in a material respect or fails to reveal a material fact that may have consequences with respect to the use of that which is advertised.

2. *Deceptive advertising* may or may not be true, but it is misleading. A deceptive advertisement could violate the ban on deceptive advertising by containing half-truths, or by being capable of several interpretations, some of which are false, or in failing to disclose important facts, which, together with what is disclosed, would lead to a different impression.

3. *Unfair advertising* is advertising that may be truthful, but offends public policy. An example would be advertising cigarettes to minors. Other violations might be advertising products that are immoral, unethical, oppressive, or unscrupulous, or the advertising of products that cause injury to consumers.

The FTC has special authority to regulate the advertising of food, pharmaceuticals, and cosmetics, although prescription drugs fall under the authority of another federal agency, the Food and Drug Administration (FDA). FDA rules for prescription drugs require that any advertising contain the name of the drug, the chemical formula for it, and medical information about its safe use.

As in many nations, the use of tobacco and liquor is considered to be a health problem in the United States. These health concerns are considered sufficient justification for severe restrictions on the advertising of tobacco and liquor products. Other special requirements are applied to these products as well, such as special labeling requirements for the packaging.

Few legal requirements restrict the advertising of cinema productions, recorded music, and video games. The industries involved with these products wish to avoid government intervention in their promotional schemes. They have joined to head off any need for official regulation by adopting voluntary guidelines for their advertising. In particular, they have adopted standards to classify their products according to their suitability for different age groups. Under the auspices of industry associations, most producers of such material have agreed among themselves to disclose the classification, or rating, in all advertising. This type of scheme is called self-regulation and is widely used in other parts of the world as shall be described.

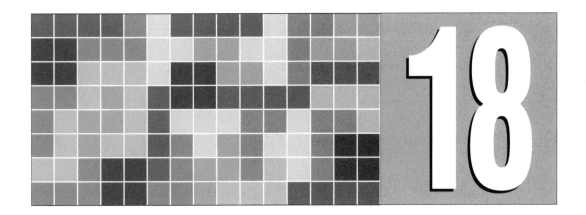

A Visit to the Regulation of Advertising in Western Europe

Just as with many other types of activities in Western Europe today, national regulation of advertising is subject to standards set in Brussels.

The 1992 reforms of the European Union included an agreement to standardize advertising regulations throughout the community. The basic framework was later set out in the 1984 European Directive on Misleading Advertising (EDMA). The definition of advertising in the EDMA is quite broad, as follows:

> The making of a representation in any form in connection with a trade, business, craft or profession in order to promote the supply of goods or services, including immovable property, rights and obligations.

Member states are required to take steps to prohibit misleading advertising defined as follows:

> Any advertising which in any way, including its presentation, deceives or is likely to deceive the persons to whom it is addressed or whom it reaches and which, by reason of its deceptive nature, is likely to affect their economic behavior or which, for those reasons, injures or is likely to injure a competitor.

The directive requires member states to make a remedy available to their citizens, either by empowering injured parties to sue the guilty advertiser directly, or by setting up an administrative authority to accept and prosecute complaints. When legal action is taken, the directive, in addition to any remedies permitted under the member's national laws, suggest three remedies.

1. The authorities may order the cessation of the misleading advertising.

2. The authorities may require publication of the decision.

3. The authorities may require the guilty party to publish a correction.

The directive does allow those European nations that already have a system of voluntary self-regulation to continue using it, but each nation must have a legal remedy in place as a backup if voluntary self-regulation fails to do the job.

The EDMA reverses the burden of proof from what had been previously used in deceptive advertising litigation. The burden is now on the advertiser to prove that its advertising is not deceptive. If it cannot meet this burden, the advertising is presumed to be deceptive. This sort of burden has particular dangers in such products as pharmaceuticals where the effectiveness of a medicine may be difficult to demonstrate objectively. If one advertises a drug in Europe today, one had better be able to back up advertised claims of safety and effectiveness with convincing scientific studies.

The EDMA provides only minimum standards for protection of consumers from deceptive advertising in the European Union. Individual EU members are free to adopt stricter national standards if they wish.

In the past, many European countries have not permitted comparative advertising. In other words, advertising in which the attributes of one product are directly compared to the attributes of a competitor's was prohibited. Those nations that did allow comparisons often still prohibited any advertisement in which the competitor is specifically named (i.e., a claim such as "a new Ford pickup truck has more leg room than the comparable Chevrolet"). The European Union is attempting to liberalize advertising regulations and has issued a 1997 directive that allows such advertising in some circumstances if it is not misleading. However, a number of restrictions still cover comparative advertising. Specific comparisons are not permitted as freely as they are in the United States.

Some restrictions on comparative advertising remain in the European Union, and a few important ones merit further description. European comparative ads must only compare goods intended for the same purpose or of the same type. Any representation of quality must be verifiable. It is not permitted to denigrate trade names or trademarks, nor is it permitted to claim that a good is an excellent replica of another branded product.

Within the framework of the European Union, the individual EU members have great latitude to devise their own regulatory schemes for advertising, and they have done so in divergent ways. Three basic systems are in use. The United Kingdom relies heavily on self-regulation while the more legalistic French try to do the job with codes and statutes. Scandinavia is unique in the world with its ombudsman system. All three will be examined in the following paragraphs.

The United Kingdom has almost no statutory laws regulating the use of advertising, but it does have well-developed industry associations and a complete system of self-regulation. Self-regulation is achieved largely through voluntary compliance with the British Code of Advertising Practice (BCAP), which sets out specific rules for specific industries and has general principles that apply to all advertising. The code requires all advertisements to be truthful and not offend common decency. Responsibility to consumers and the society as a whole is also required. Pharmaceuticals, cigarettes, and liquor each have their own guidelines. Enforcement of BCAP is through an independent body called the Advertising Standards Authority.

Although statutes prohibiting misleading advertising have been rare in the United Kingdom, some are being developed at present. Still, much commercial law used in the United Kingdom is actually derived from the precedent set by prior court decisions. These numerous precedents serve to regulate advertising. Under English common law, advertising is sometimes a legal offer to contract but more often considered an invitation to negotiate. In order for a company to be held to its advertising claims strictly, it must be shown that the representations made in the advertisement were so definite that someone buying the product was legally accepting a specific offer creating a contractual relationship with the seller. This situation requires the performance of the goods as represented to be a term of that sales contract. Failure of the goods to perform as promised in the advertisement then constitutes a breach of contract on the part of the seller. Thus, claims such as "This pill will absolutely cure any headache within 30 minutes" must be true. If not true, the claim may subject the seller to liability under a breach of contract theory.

The most important statutory law in the United Kingdom is the Trade Descriptions Act (TDA) of 1968, which makes it a criminal offense to falsely describe goods in advertising or to falsely advertise a price. Prosecution of such cases is by the public authorities, although citizens who are harmed by false advertising may also bring private suits for damages under the law.

Like most nations, the United Kingdom has special regulations regarding the advertising of food products and medicines.

Advertising regulations take a different form in countries based on the Romano-Germanic legal system. Quite typical of such countries is France. Advertising law there is found both in the Napoleonic code and in statutes. Little French common law is made directly by the courts as in a common law system, although the judges in France do have great latitude to interpret the code law.

Under the French civil code, deceptive advertising is considered unfair competition. It is a civil wrong, or tort, under the French civil code to make or engage in a falsehood that causes harm to a competitor or denies the competitor a potential customer. The wrong can take the form of deliberately confusing the customer, or something similar to libel when the reputation of the competitor is unfairly attacked. In the past nearly every direct comparison with a competitor was forbidden, but that restriction is changing with the adoption of the European directive discussed previously.

Misleading advertising is a crime in France. The French Penal Code directly addresses it as a statutory penal offense. In order to obtain a conviction, the prosecutor must prove that the advertising is misleading and that the advertiser acted in bad faith. French penal law contains a long list of facts that may not be misrepresented in an advertisement without risking a criminal offense. In addition to the advertiser, the advertising agency and even the media may also be prosecuted if they know of the deceptive nature of the advertising and publish it anyway.

As in most of the rest of the world, the French have strictly regulated, with specific statutes, the advertising of food, alcohol, tobacco, and pharmaceuticals.

The legal system in Scandinavian countries, like the French system, is basically Romano-Germanic in character. But regulation of advertising in Scandinavia is differentiated from that of France and other European Union countries by extensive use of the ombudsman system.

The ombudsman is an official appointed by the government who, though hired and paid by the government, operates independently of both government and business. The ombudsman's job is to be officially neutral at the outset and investigate possible deception in advertising as well as other abuse of consumers.

If an instance of deceptive advertising is discovered, the ombudsman attempts to persuade the offending business to comply with standards voluntarily while also arbitrating a solution to the dispute with any injured party. Most frequently, such matters are quickly and peacefully resolved, but not always.

If the ombudsman fails to resolve a matter by mutual agreement, the ombudsman may bring a civil action against the offending party in court. There the ombudsman's arbitration role ends and a legally binding judgment will end the matter. If criminal conduct is involved, the ombudsman may turn the matter over to the prosecutor.

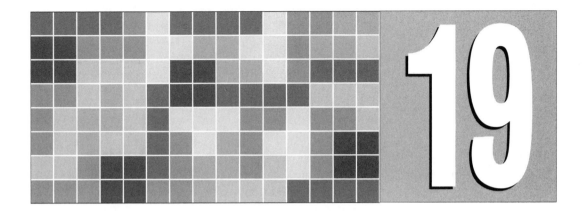

An Overview of Advertising Laws in the Rest of the World

ISLAMIC NATIONS

As one might expect in a traditional religious setting, advertising regulation in Arabia has an entirely different focus. Deception is forbidden as an affront to the teachings of Islam, and great concern focuses on this likelihood that even truthful advertising can further, or offend, Islamic principles. Therefore, any advertising that is perceived to be hostile to Islamic principles is not permitted.

One problem faced by the advertiser in Arabia, therefore, is to find media where an advertisement of a sensitive nature can be placed. Many Arab countries do not allow commercial broadcasting of the type known in the West. However, newspapers and magazines are prevalent and do welcome advertising, and so print may be the medium of choice.

Although many Arab nations severely restrict the type of advertising that may be placed in those newspapers and journals produced within their borders, many do allow the free importation of jounals from other Islamic countries. Some of these other journals may be from Arab countries that have more liberal advertising policies. These pan-Arab journals provide a backdoor to advertise such things as pharmaceuticals and cosmetics in countries where access to the local media is denied.

Islam is friendly to the conduct of private business for profit. Commercial speech is not generally held in disdain so advertising may be done quite freely if it is kept within the parameters imposed by Islam. Those parameters, mostly religious and moral in character, are quite strictly enforced.

Islam forbids the consumption of pork so the advertising of pork products is prohibited. Likewise, no advertising of alcoholic beverages is permitted. The use of pharmaceuticals to cure disease or relieve suffering is permitted by most Islamic thinking, but advertising that encourages their use is not considered good public policy and is restrained or prohibited in many Arab countries. Some Arab countries are more liberal than others in this regard, so the pan-Arab journals as already discussed may provide a solution to the business that wishes to advertise a headache remedy in Arabia.

In places where they are permitted at all, advertisements for any sort of pharmaceutical product must usually be approved in advance of publication by a government agency. Most Arab countries restrict, in some way, the advertising of tobacco.

The use of images of women in advertising can be a minefield for the foreign businessperson in Arabia. A strong reaction can result when a woman is presented in an immodest manner or in any way that suggests that she is anything other than a dedicated mother, good wife, and devoted to Islam.

It is almost a blessing in Arabia that a censor, before publication, must often screen advertising. This practice allows cultural problems to be identified and corrected before the populace has an opportunity to associate some undesirable trait with one's product. In Islamic countries where prior clearance is not required, it might be advisable to show any proposed advertising to a respected religious leader prior to publication. His favorable opinion as to acceptability is a good defense to any subsequent charge of cultural or religious insensitivity.

LATIN AMERICA

Latin American is in a period in transition. In previous times many governments there tried to own many business activities directly. The businesses that governments did not own they often tried to overcontrol with extremely burdensome government regulation, including regulation of advertising. Such regulation multiplied throughout the 1970s and into the

1980s. In order to encourage the development of a local advertising industry, many Latin American countries adopted laws prohibiting the use of foreign-produced advertising.

Applying traditional Romano-Germanic law inherited from the Spanish and Portuguese, most Latin American nations use a system of regulation based on civil and criminal law similar to that of France. In the Latin America of past decades, a cumbersome and often corrupt bureaucracy, using regulation and consumer protection legislation to harass and seek bribes from private interests, often made a nightmare of the business climate for both foreign and domestic business. Obviously such a climate exacted a toll on the economies of the region. In the 1990s the bill for such bad policy came due, and new foreign investment diminished in the face of such a hostile business climate.

These bureaucratic, top-heavy, centrally managed economies have fallen like economic dominoes in the face of globalization during the last few years. Out of the ashes of economic collapse, destitution, and debt came may positive changes, however.

The recent trend in Latin America has been to privatize state-owned businesses, reduce bureaucracy, and deregulate business in order to encourage new investment and economic growth. Unfortunately, the advertising industry did not benefit from this era of deregulation as much as did other business activities, and the regulation of advertising in most of Latin America remains quite burdensome.

The number of nations in Latin America makes it impractical to discuss them one by one in this chapter. It shall be sufficient to say that advertising in Latin America remains heavily regulated, particularly in the name of consumer protection. A movement is afoot to replace government involvement in advertising regulation in Latin America with new systems of self-regulation. The change is overdue but is currently still in the future.

JAPAN AND CHINA

Japan uses self-regulation combined with formal regulation. False or misleading advertising has been prohibited by statute since 1908. The Japanese first adopted an entire advertising code in 1940. After the Second World War, a new law regulating many aspects of private business called the Act Concerning Prohibition of Private Monopoly and Maintenance of Fair Trade was adopted. It addresses the issue of deceptive advertising and, with several amendments, remains Japan's most comprehensive advertising regulation law. In a nutshell, the act forbids inducing a sale through misrepresentation or coercion. Enforcement of the law is through Japan's Fair Trade Commission (FTC).

The commission's enforcement style is a bit different from that of regulatory agencies in the West. When the Japanese FTC detects a violation it may issue a warning, or it may order an end to the use of the offending advertisement (an abatement). If abatement is ordered, the offending company must publicize the fact that they have violated the law causing embarrassment and loss of face for the offending company. The offender must also make a report to the FTC documenting its violation. For the entire subsequent year, advertisers who have been ordered an abatement must submit their proposed new advertising to the FTC for approval before publication or broadcasting. Fines, so commonly used in the West, are not used in Japan for ordinary deceptive advertising cases and the FTC does not publicize such cases, though they are ordered publicized by the offender.

As described in the chapter on the Japanese legal system, the Japanese prefer to avoid legal solutions to problems. In order to avoid official action, Japanese business has developed a comprehensive system of self-regulation called the Japan Advertising Review Organization (JARO). The JARO privately reviews advertising complaints and mediates disputes over advertising. The JARO is not an official agency but it has a good relationship with the FTC. Often the FTC does not involve itself in cases that are being resolved through the auspices of the JARO.

China has a fairly well-developed body of law regulating advertising but, consistent with the Confucian policy of avoiding the conflict of legalism, it is not readily applied. China's principle advertising law is known as the Regulations for Advertising Management. In a couple of pages, the text defines what is allowed in advertising, sets forth penalities for violations, and suggests self-regulation. It is vague and its requirements uncertain. But because it is a law of China, it is probably not meant to be used much anyway.

The diversity of requirements and cultural pitfalls around the world make it advisable for the advertiser to seek advice from experienced locals before designing and executing an advertising campaign in a foreign country.

SECTION VI

A Panorama of Treaties Affecting International Commerce

Treaties and conventions are agreements between nations to conduct their relations and treat each other in a defined way in the future.

A treaty is based on the premise that all of its parties are sovereign nations and legally equal. Therefore a treaty, like a contract, has some measure of give and take, and the nature of the exchange determines the classifications or standard of the treaty. Countries use a number of treaty standards, and the most common will be described in this section.

1. *Most Favored Nation:* When a nation makes a treaty based on most favored nation (MFN) status, it grants the other party the same rights that the nation already grants those nations with whom it enjoys good relations. The name, which suggests special treatment, is misleading because most favored nation status usually confers rights that are normally granted to most any friendly nation. The rights granted to MFN nations are usually denied only to those perceived as enemies or competitors.

2. *National Standard:* A treaty based on the national standard is usually an agreement whereby nations agree to treat each other's citizens the same as they treat their own with respect to the subject of the treaty. Thus, if two nations establish a national standard with respect to investment,

they agree that the other nation's citizens may make investments in the country on the same basis as the citizens of the country.

3. *Standard of Mutuality:* In this literal application, a nation agrees to do something with respect to the other if the same favor is returned. An example would be if a nation offered to drop a visa requirements from visiting tourists from another country if the other country would do the same for tourists from the offering country.

4. *Preferential Treatment:* This type of treaty offers discrimination in favor of those who agree to the treaty. Good examples are regional trade blocs such as NAFTA or the European Union. These treaties require members to offer the other members lower tariff rates—frequently no tariff at all—than the members give anyone else.

A number of important international agreements affect international business. Some impose serious hazards and others confer advantages. The international businessperson should be aware of their existence. This section will discuss a few of the most important.

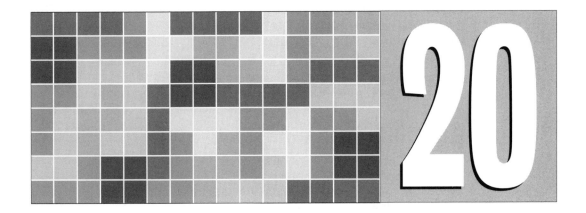

An Expedition to the World of Commercial Treaties

COCOM AND ITS SUCCESSORS

Formally known as the Coordinating Committee for Multilateral Export Controls, COCOM is a treaty forming a consortium of European countries and the United States. It is designed to prevent military or economic benefits from reaching enemies through restriction on exports.

The United States has long restricted export of sensitive materials. Export controls have been widely used since the early twentieth century to limit arms and military technology transfer to potential and actual enemies. In fact, the first use of export controls took place even before the United States became a nation when the government of the insurrection banned exports to Britain.

Extensive restrictions were put into place during the Second World War. After the world war ended, the cold war soon began. In 1949, the export of certain military products to Communist countries was prohibited. That same year, the United States and a number of European nations together with Australia and New Zealand joined together to form COCOM. In the COCOM agreement, the members agreed to prohibit their citizens from exporting arms and arms technology to Communist countries.

COCOM was enforced in the United States through legislation called the Mutual Defense Assistance Act adopted in 1951. The controls were modified and strengthened by further legislation in 1954, in 1962 after the Cuban Missile Crisis, and in 1969, 1974, and 1977. Some thought the rules were too strict and that the United States and other members of COCOM were losing export revenue unnecessarily. In 1979 the United States enacted Export Administration Act, which set up a system for balancing the economic costs of export controls with national security interests.

As the cold war ended, many of the restrictions on Communist countries were eased, and the COCOM agreement ended by its terms in 1994. Although the agreement has expired, legislation based on the agreement remains in effect in many of the former member countries. Consequently, a study of that law is necessary before exports from former member nations are contemplated. A new agreement was formed in 1996 called the Wassenaar Arrangement. This arrangement does not have the teeth that COCOM did. It merely requires that when a nation decides to make a controversial export it gives notice to the others. Despite the lack of an enforcement mechanism, the Wassenaar Arrangement does have 33 members. The required notice must be given, and most of the members require export licenses and may deny them if a security threat to the whole is perceived.

Any discussion about export controls must make mention of the fact that export controls are tricky to design. The idea is to not to restrict exports unless a national security problem is involved. The controls only work when all sources of the desired product refuse to export it. If other willing sources are available to the forbidden nation, the controls only serve to direct potentially profitable business away from the country imposing the controls.

At present, the state of national and international law concerning export controls is in a state of flux. It is sufficient for this basic survey if the student or businessperson knows that such controls exist and understands that the current state of the law should be determined before any commitment is formed to make a shipment that could subject one to a civil action or criminal prosecution.

CISG

The United Nations Convention of Contracts for the International Sale of Goods (CISG) is the world's commercial code for international sales. Although not a particularly good code in the opinion of some, the CISG is useful in one important aspect. It defines what is the law when a question arises about whose law applies to a situation.

Consider the following sales transaction. The contract is signed in Switzerland. The buyer is from India and intends to import the product into the United Kingdom. The seller is Turkish and represents a manufacturer in Southern Russia. The goods are to be flown from Russia in crates, which were produced in the Philippines, to Istanbul on a Greek airline that has an interline agreement with a French airline for the final hop to London. The goods arrive damaged and it is unclear whether the damage occurred in transit or before, or was the result of defective manufacture, defective crates, negligent handling, or perhaps fraud on the part of the buyer and no damage at all. All these issues must be sorted out, and whose sales law applies? Russian? Turkish? Philippine? British? Greek? Indian? Swiss? French? If the contract is silent about what nation's law is to be applied, a horrendous lawsuit that takes months or years of litigation only serves to determine the law to be used before any of the issues involved are even considered. The legal costs of such a suit probably exceed the value of the goods in question. The CISG is designed to end that sort of problem, although it might not apply to the preceding situation because some of the nations involved have not ratified it.

The CISG applies to contracts for the commercial sale of goods if the sale is between parties whose places of business are in different nations that have ratified the CISG. The CISG does not apply to a number of transactions, however. The most important exceptions are consumer goods sold for personal use, securities, contracts preponderantly for labor, contracts for the sale of ships, and contracts that include a clause that the CISG does not apply.

A contract is formed under the CISG if the parties mutually agree to be contractually bound and legal consideration is given on both sides, the parties are legally able to enter into a contract, and the purpose of the contract is legal.

The CISG differs in many ways from the body of contract law, as it is normally understood in the United States. These differences can lead to some problems, so a few of the differences will be discussed here.

- The CISG holds no requirement that a sales contract must be in writing.

- The CISG does not recognize the parole evidence rule, in other words, the rule that restricts the modification of a written contract with an oral agreement. Under the CISG, the parties may introduce testimony that oral agreements were made that conflict with the written version of the contract.

- No definite price has to be decided upon for a contract to be formed under the CISG. If the parties agree to sell and buy, but no price is named, the court will determine a market price and apply it.

- Silence can sometimes be construed as an acceptance of a contract offer under the CISG.

One of the most troublesome aspects of the CISG is the provision that contracts are to be interpreted according not to the clear meaning of the words, but rather in the context of the culture of the person sought to be held to the contract. Obviously this culture test opens the door for a party to claim that a clear statement means something else in that party's culture. Proving or disproving the effect of a foreign culture on the perception of its adherents introduces an element of uncertainty to a contract that otherwise seems crystal clear on its surface.

Although the CISG solves the conflict of law problem nicely, it was written with input from many nations. Some of them are socialist. Others are hostile to private business, or not members of the group of experienced commercial countries. The CISG is not particularly good sales law from the viewpoint of a private company based in a well-developed country. The application of the CISG should be generally avoided by the express adoption of another body of law in the sales contract.

WARSAW CONVENTION

The Warsaw Convention governs the activities of international air carriers with respect to their liability for loss of cargo, including baggage, and injury to passengers. It also provides requirements for the bills of lading used by air carriers called "air waybills."

The rule of liability in the event of damaged cargo is simple. The burden of proof with regard to fault is on the carrier if damage occurs to cargo. The carrier is liable to pay for any damage unless the carrier can prove that it was not at fault. The carrier has a defense if the damage was due to the negligence of the shipper in handling, packaging, or marking the goods. Absent one of these defenses, that the carrier was not at fault at all, or the shipper caused the problem by improper shipping techniques, the carrier must pay for damage up to the limits imposed by the convention.

However, the limit for the carrier's liability is quite low, having been fixed at $9.07 ($US) per pound. This low limit is a result of the treaty being originally based on the price of gold. When the United States went off the gold standard in the 1970s, the limit was based on the last official price of gold, and has not been raised since.

CARRIAGE OF GOODS BY SEA ACT

Although not a treaty, the U. S. Carriage of Goods by Sea Act (COGSA) is a codified version of the Hague Convention. The purpose of the Hague Convention is to standardize the world's law on a cargo ship operator's liability to the cargo owners. Many shipping companies specify the COGSA as the applicable law for their bills of lading because COGSA is quite favorable to the shipping company and, of course, bills of lading, which specify applicable law, are prepared by shipping companies and not shippers.

COGSA gives shippers of cargo that is damaged only one year to file any claim. After that the law bars a claim for damage to cargo. Liability under the COGSA is much more difficult to establish against an ocean carrier than is the case with air cargo under the Warsaw Convention. With the COGSA, the vessel's operator only has the duty to make certain the vessel is reasonably fit to do the job it is hired for, in other words "seaworthy." A seaworthy ship is one about which the carrier has used due diligence to ascertain that it was in good condition and had the proper equipment to transport the type of cargo contracted for. Due diligence is also required on the part of the vessel's operator to ascertain that the crew is reasonably competent and, if it is done by the carrier, the goods are properly loaded and stowed. If the carrier meets this test of due diligence it will not usually be held liable for any damage that occurs to the cargo even if the crew's negligence is the cause.

If any loss occurs, the shipper only has to prove that the loss occurred in order to establish the initial case. The burden then shifts to the carrier to prove that it used due diligence as already described. Sixteen specific defenses to liability protect the ship owner from any liability if one of the defensible occurrences was the cause of the loss.

1. Error in navigation or management of the ship

2. Fire, unless caused by the fault of the corporate owner of the ship (as opposed to say, the crew)

3. Perils, dangers, and accidents of the sea (such as lightening or an unpredicted storm)

4. An act of God or natural disaster (such as a tidal wave)

5. An act of war

6. An act of public enemies (such as piracy)

7. Legal seizure of the ship

8. Quarantine restrictions

9. Act or omission of the owner of the goods or shipper

10. Labor strikes

11. Riots or civil commotions

12. Saving life or property at sea

13. Inherent waste, quality, or defect in the goods that causes wastage (such as cookies spoiling after several days)

14. Insufficiency of packing

15. Inadequate marking of the goods or containers (such as frozen meat, which should be marked in a way that it is obvious that it must be kept frozen)

16. Latent defects in the ship or machinery that were not discoverable by due diligence

If the carrier has no defense, despite the many escapes available to it in the law, the amount of money it must pay for damage to cargo is limited. It can be no more than $500 ($US) per package unless the shipper declares a higher value on the bill of lading and therefore accepts a higher shipping rate. A myriad of litigation has been brought over what constitutes a "package" for purposes of the COGSA. For example, suppose an intermodal container is lost overboard. The container held 175 crates, and each crate contains four automobile transmissions, each in its own box. Is each transmission a package or is the container itself the only package? Liability of the carrier for the loss will vary from only $500 to as much as $35,000 depending on the court's answer, and the COGSA is not clear on such questions.

Rather than take a chance on the application of the COGSA, the shipper should obtain an insurance policy for valuable cargo, which, if lost, could cause the company an unbearable financial loss.

THE PARIS CONVENTION

Formally known as the International Convention for the Protection of Industrial Property, but universally referred to as the Paris Convention, this agreement guarantees national treatment, such as the privileges a nation grants to its own citizens, to foreign applicants for trademark protection and patents. National treatment is often an inadequate standard however.

Courts of many nations that harbor no pharmaceutical research capability have, in the past, ruled that patent protection of pharmaceuticals was immoral due to the effect of raising the cost of drugs that alleviate suffering. With no nationally developed drugs, no local producer suffered from the resultant right to produce pharmaceutical formulas of another nation's companies royalty free.

The Paris convention also has no convenient enforcement mechanism, which also makes it less than satisfactory to owners of intellectual property rights.

BERNE CONVENTION

The Berne Convention for the Protection of Literary and Artistic Works provides a national treatment scheme for the protection of rights to original art and literature. In 1996 computer programs were added to the list of types of property that could be protected by this agreement. The Berne Convention is more effective than the Paris Convention in that it requires signatory nations to adopt minimum standards of protection.

A number of regional agreements address intellectual property protection and in the interest of brevity, not all are discussed here. Some of the more important ones can be found as part of the structure of the World Trade Organization and as part of the structure of the European Union. However, the World Trade Organization is so complex and is of such profound importance to international business that it has its own chapter in this book.

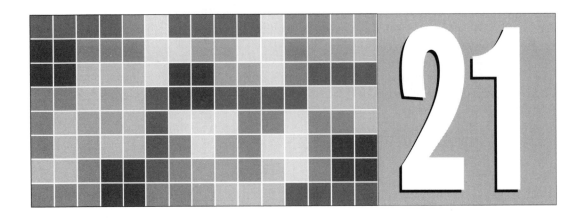

An Expedition to the World Trade Organization

The WTO is not a trade boc, but it is important and is discussed here because it is an attempt to make the whole world one large trading bloc.

To understand the WTO, some historical perspective is necessary. Between the two world wars, many nations, including the United States, adopted the policy of protecting their domestic industries from competition abroad by various schemes on tariff and nontariff barriers to imports.

Unfortunately the United States led the world down a dangerous path with the passage of the Smoot-Hawley Act of 1930. It raised tariffs to extremely high levels just as the United States was entering the Great Depression. Other nations retaliated against the United States by enacting their own high tariffs against foreign goods. As a result, international trade volume in the whole world dropped precipitously, aggravating the effects of the Great Depression. The economic cataclysm that followed is widely considered to be one of the factors in the deepening of the depression as well as a cause of the Second World War.

The Allied powers did not wish to go down the world warpath a third time, so conferences were set up to guide world affairs when the fighting was over. At a conference in Yalta, the United Nations was created. Trade and economic matters were considered at a conference at Bretton Woods, New Hampshire, in 1944. At Bretton Woods, the World Bank and the International Monetary Fund were conceived, and a global scheme to regulate trade and tariffs to prevent another Smoot-Hawley fiasco was envisioned. This new organization was to be called the International Trade Organization (ITO). The World Bank and International Monetary Fund were quickly realized but an international organization to regulate trade fell victim to opposition focused in the United States.

The failure to put an international trade organization in place did not stop the world from working on the reduction of trade barriers. In 1947, many of the world's trading nations agreed on a multilateral tariff treaty that restricted their rights to engage in Smoot-Hawley–style trade competition. This treaty was called the General Agreement on Trade and Tariffs, or GATT. GATT put restrictions on discriminatory tariffs that set rates for goods of some nations higher than for others. These restrictions did not apply to trade between different members of major trading blocs such as the European Union. The GATT also provided a forum for negotiations to reduce or remove tariff and nontariff barriers to trade. But the GATT was inherently weak because it had no underlying organization to enforce it.

A second attempt to form a world trade organization took place in 1955 when the GATT members tried to form the Organization for Trade Cooperation. This effort failed, again probably as a result of the lack of support from the United States.

But despite the lack of a worldwide organization, the GATT continued to grow in membership, and by 1995, 128 nations were signatories to the GATT agreement. In the course of years, five further rounds of negotiations were held, all of which successfully reduced some tariffs. In addition, the Kennedy round in the 1960s added an agreement that nations could do something about dumping.

Dumping is the exporting of goods at lower prices than are charged in the domestic market in order to build market share. Many nations consider dumping a threat to their domestic producers and wish to curtail dumping activities.

The Tokyo round in the 1970s attempted to reduce the barriers to trade that do not take the form of tariffs. These nontariff barriers can be quotas on the total amount that can be imported or bureaucratic burdens of various types and regulations that discriminate against foreign products.

The overall weaknesses in the GATT agreement were readily apparent, however. It had no enforcement mechanism and no good mechanism to resolve disputes. These shortcomings clearly had to be addressed if world trade was to be truly regulated according to international agreement.

An agreement was made in 1986 for GATT to negotiate new agreement in a series of conferences called the Uruguay Round. This series lasted eight years (1986 to 1994) and resulted in the Marrakesh agreement that is the framework of the present World Trade Organization (WTO), headquartered in Geneva, Switzerland. The WTO extended the scope of GATT to include areas not previously regulated such as trade in services and intellectual property. The GATT had previously only dealt with trade goods. The functions of the WTO were defined as follow:

- Administering WTO trade agreements

- Providing a forum for trade negotiations

- Handling trade disputes

- Monitoring national trade policies

- Technical assistance and training for developing countries

- Cooperating with other international organizations.

After the formation of the WTO, negotiations continued to lead to agreements on telecommunications services and to remove tariffs on high-technology products in many countries.

The WTO has continued the work of the GATT, reducing tariffs to generally low levels and reducing nontariff barriers. In addition, the WTO has a grievance procedure with some teeth in it, which has already worked to peacefully and definitively resolve a number of serious trade disputes. The WTO has also made great strides to include agricultural products and textiles in the trade scheme. These products were theoretically covered by the GATT but were the subject of so many loopholes as to be effectively unregulated.

The GATT did not cover trade in services, only goods. Along with the adoption of the WTO came a General Agreement on Trade in Services (GATT), which included this trade for the first time in the world's trade regulation system. Also, the GATT did not regulate trade in intellectual property such as patents, trademarks, and copyrights. As a result, nations where piracy was rampant were not subject to any consequences. This issue too has been remedied under the WTO. A number of the other changes resulted from the WTO, but the greatest was perhaps that now an organization had as its purpose the enforcement of the agreements.

The GATT and WTO have been successful by many different measures. The world has had a relatively stable trading system since adoption of the GATT and world trade has grown enormously. Merchandise trade has grown an average of 6 percent per year since the GATT was adopted, and before the first 50 years of the new order in trade, the world total had grown by more than 14 times. As of 2000, WTO membership had increased to 136 nations.

The inception of the WTO in 1995 meant that the world's trade was overseen for the first time by an intergovernmental organization whose purpose was to make the trade process smoother and freer. For smaller countries, the advantages in belonging to the WTO are that the same rules apply to everyone, big or small. The small nations are not discriminated against. In fact, the WTO requires, in many cases, that each member grant other members most favored nation status, which means that they must treat all their trading partners the same regardless of size or politics. Trade between nations belonging to regional trading agreements is an exception from this requirement however. Under the WTO, large countries have the advantage of having one overall scheme to govern their trade throughout the world, which relieves them from having separate arrangements with all the many countries they deal with.

A number of areas are particularly important to world trade under the auspices of the WTO.

RULES FOR EVALUATING GOODS AT CUSTOMS

Of what use is it to know that a tarif cannot exceed 5 percent of value under WTO agreements, only to have the customs service of the importing country set value at an arbitrarily high figure? To solve this problem, the WTO has an agreement on customs valuation that aims to make value a function of the commercial reality rather than the whim of a government official.

Some nations, particularly developing countries, require that incoming shipments be inspected before shipment by a private company to check price, quality, and quantity presumably as a safeguard against evasion of duties or fraud. In practice, inspections may serve as nontariff barriers to complicate the important process in order to protect domestic industry. Inspections might also be a way to compel business to be steered to licensed "inspectors" who are really just friends of government officials in the receiving countries. This agreement adopts rules to restrict abuses of the pre-shipment inspection process.

AGREEMENT ON RULES OF ORIGIN

Nations are still allowed to discriminate, favoring some foreign goods at the expense of others. For example, some nations are not members of the WTO. Goods brought from them are not subject to WTO restrictions on tariffs. Other goods may be bought from regional trading blocs and also not subject to WTO regulations. What nation is the origin of a good? The answer may be more complicated than appears on the surface. A good may be assembled in one country from parts imported from a second country, which parts are made from materials imported from a third country. The whole thing may then be placed in a package produced in a fourth country and so forth. This agreement prohibits origin rules that are not easy to understand and apply and those that have the effect of causing economic distortions to trade.

ANTIDUMPING AND ANTISUBSIDY AGREEMENTS

Two problems that have plagued international business are addressed by the antidumping and antisubsidy agreements.

1. If an industry has a good capital base, one competitive strategy might be to flood a foreign market with goods priced below the prevailing market price in order to keep prices so low that all competitors lose hope of profitability and drop out of the business. Then, free of competition, tremendous profits may be realized. If export goods are priced below the price that is charged in the country where the goods are manufactured it is called dumping.

2. A government might find it to be good politics, if questionable economics, to pay government subsidies to an unprofitable exporting industry. Although this tactic has been shown to be an enormously expensive way to preserve jobs, some nations do engage in subsidizing exports. These techniques are obviously considered unfair by the nations whose industries are destroyed or whose workers are laid off as a result of the other nation's dumping and subsidies. The antidumping and antisubsidy agreements are intended to correct this problem and provide the victims a remedy. These agreements consist of a set of rules for calculating the amount of dumping, detailed procedures gathering evidence of dumping, and procedures for the imposition of antidumping measures.

In the case of subsidies, the agreement on that topic gives member nations the choice of using the WTO's dispute mechanism, or the imposing of countervailing tariffs on the subsidized goods to neutralize the economic effect of the subsidies. The agreement also specifies which types of subsidies are prohibited and which are not.

TRADE POLICY REVIEW MECHANISM

Prior to WTO, international trade was a rat's nest of interwoven national regulations, and to a great extent it still is. Worse, the regulations are subject to change at the whim of the members, making the trade process unnecessarily complex. The members of the WTO have attempted to remedy this problem with trade policy review agreements that require a nation to inform fellow WTO members of pending changes in their trade regulation. The WTO conducts periodic surveys of its members' trade policies. The largest trading countries are examined on a biannual basis. The rest are surveyed every 4 or 6 years, depending on their size. The result is published in a series of regular reports comparing the nation's standards to the world's, thereby making the trade process easier and more transparent.

DISPUTE RESOLUTION MECHANISM

In the first 5 years of the WTO's existence, almost 200 international trade disputes have been handled by the organization. About half of the disputes are settled between the parties without the need for a WTO ruling. The rest are resolved through binding arbitration. This ability to resolve such disputes definitively and peacefully is a blessing to the world.

The WTO also grants a forum to nations that would have formerly been powerless to stand up to the big powers. Fifty of the first 194 disputes were filed by developing countries. The United States has, however, filed the largest number of complaints. The European Union is the second most prolific filer of complaints.

INTELLECTUAL PROPERTY PROTECTION AND ENFORCEMENT

Intellectual property, consisting of design and technology patents, trademarks, logos, and copyrights, is important to the nations that produce goods that have intellectual property as a large part of their value. For example, it may cost only a few cents each to produce a tablet of a certain medicine as a chemical compound. The research that discovered the compound and proved it safe and effective may have cost hundreds of millions of dollars. It is argued in many nations that such investment should be rewarded by patent protection giving the developer of a new pharmaceutical an exclusive right to profit from it for a fixed number of years. The WTO supports the viewpoint that a nation should apply its rules for the protection of intellectual property equally to its own nationals and foreigners.

The WTO agreement on intellectual property requires that foreign interests receive national treatment under a nation's intellectual scheme. That is, a foreign holder of an intellectual property interest should receive the same treatment as a domestic one. The WTO also prescribes most favored nation treatment for the holder of intellectual property. In other words, if a nation protects intellectual property from one WTO member it must apply the same protection to all WTO members.

Intellectual property protection varies widely from country to country. In order to standardize intellectual property rights somewhat, many WTO members have agreed to respect two agreements of the World Intellectual Property Organization.

1. *The Paris Convention:* In this international agreement, nations agree to respect the rights of the nationals of other countries with regard to design and technology patents.

2. *The Berne Convention:* In this international agreement, nations agree to respect copyrights originating in other nations.

The WTO itself has set ground rules for computer programs, integrated circuit designs, trade secrets, sound recordings, live performances, and film. It has set a 20-year minimum for patent protection. These types of intellectual property are not adequately covered by other international agreements.

TARIFFS

Since the beginning, under the auspices of the WTO's forerunner the GATT, tariff reductions have been a top priority of the organization. Great cuts in tariffs were negotiated before the WTO was formed in 1995, and the average tariff for industrial goods in the world at the formation of the WTO was about 6.3 percent. That rate has now been reduced to 3.8 percent. In fact, about 40 percent of industrial products traded in the world today receive duty-free treatment. The world is rapidly approaching a point where tariffs will not be a significant factor in international competition.

INTERNATIONAL TRADE IN SERVICES

The GATT had no provisions to regulate trade in services. The addition of such agreements was a major accomplishment of the Uruguay round and the WTO. The General Agreement on Trade in Services covers all internationally traded services. These services may take any of four forms:

1. *Cross-Border Supply Services:* These services originate in one country and are used in another, such as an aircraft-based overnight delivery service.

2. *Consumption:* This type of service usually involves travel to a foreign country to take advantage of a service offered there, such as visiting a medical doctor in a neighboring country where the needed medical specialty is available.

3. *Commercial Presence:* In this situation, a company sets up a branch in a foreign country to render services in that location.

4. *Presence of Natural Persons:* Professional business people, professional sports players, consultants, fashion models, or others sometimes travel to a foreign country to render a service. In each of these areas the nation must give the foreign-based service provider most favored nation treatment. It may not discriminate between service providers of different foreign countries. Note that national treatment is not required as it is for trade in goods.

NONTARIFF BARRIERS

Suppose a nation wants the benefits of WTO membership in order to easily export its products, but doesn't want to open its markets to foreign competitors. As a member of the WTO, it cannot raise tariffs. But it could try to raise many other types of barriers to imports. For example it could require that a product be made of a type of wood that only grows within its borders although many other types of wood could serve just as well. Or it could require a safety inspection and conveniently have the inspector declare all foreign products to be unsafe.

To avoid such abuses, the WTO promulgates the Agreement on Technical Barriers to Trade. It speaks to health and safety standards, regulations, testing, and certification procedures.

The agreement permits countries to adopt the standards and procedures it deems appropriate. Use of international standards, where they exist, are encouraged. The main point is that the same standards should apply to domestic and imported goods. Member nations are required to provide information on their standards to potential importers through a national enquiry point.

In recent years the WTO has been under attack by a number of groups with various political agendas. The overall success of the organization, however, in facilitating greatly increased world trade cannot be denied.

SECTION VII

A Guidebook for International Business Transactions

The process of expanding a business abroad entails a multitude of choices in method. Each of the many ways to enter the international marketplace carries its own risks and potential rewards. Choosing the best way, and reviewing that decision when conditions change, is the responsibility of management. Because regulatory and tax considerations are an important factor in this decision, the managers are usually aided by legal counsel.

Marketing one's products abroad can be divided into two wide, and often overlapping, categories. Both are flourishing areas of business expansion, but for practical reasons this book shall present an overview of only one.

The first category is the marketing of services. This area is often strictly regulated, and the regulations vary greatly from country to country. The regulations affecting international marketing of services are so diverse that they do not lend themselves to explanation in a book of this type. Understanding the factors in the marketing of services usually requires a careful law-by-law search of the home and target nations' laws to ensure that each aspect of the operation is in compliance. An exception might be the European Union. The EU is in the process of developing a standardized legal base to facilitate EU-based operations in efforts to market services in fellow EU member nations. In general though, it is not possible to summarize the regulations for the international marketing of services. Changes may be in the works now that the WTO has taken up the cause of reducing barriers to trade in services. Perhaps meaningful rules will be adopted and future editions of this book may have a chapter on that subject.

The other category is the marketing of physical goods. Although individual countries have their own regulations, some standardization exists thanks to a number of international agreements and customs.

Of the various ways to get one's goods into a foreign market, the easiest is simply producing a few more at home and shipping them to the foreign market for sale—in other words, exporting. Particularly when using excess production capacity, exporting has the advantage of requiring little in the way of capital investment, long-term commitment, or other risk. Weighed against this low risk level are disadvantages such as shipping, customs duties, extra packaging, paperwork, freight forwarding, customs brokerage, permits, inspections, delays reaching the market, and a multitude of other expenses and problems that are detrimental to profitability.

We could license a foreign producer to manufacture our goods for us and sell them in its home and other nearby countries using our name or technology. That strategy could avoid most of the extra expenses associated with transportation and crossing borders, and we would have the help of a local business, which would presumably understand the problems associated with doing business in that place and the idiosyncrasies of the local market. Our investment would still be quite low. But profitability might be limited because the foreign manufacturer would expect to share any proceeds. If we license, we might also have undesirable consequence of teaching a future competitor about our business. If we are to license abroad we must understand the system for protection of foreign investors, the subject of the last chapter.

Finally, we could manufacture or sell our goods abroad through our own foreign venture: purchasing a place of business, obtaining necessary permits and licenses, hiring or bringing in employees, and operating in the foreign country on basically the same basis as a company domiciled there. This method entails great risk. First, it requires a large capital outlay and ongoing operating expenses that must all be borne by the home company until the investment achieves profitability. We will be operating in a foreign environment with attendant tax, regulatory, labor, and cultural problems that may be difficult to anticipate and plan for. But with great risk may come great rewards. If this venture is successful we will realize all the profits, perhaps without the extra expenses associated with exporting.

Sometimes an attempt is made to reduce the risks of such a direct investment by taking on a local partner who advances some of the capital and provides local knowledge. In the past, many nations required local partners before they would allow foreigners to invest, though the trend today is to encourage investments by abolishing such requirements. Even though such joint ventures sound good in theory, these arrangements frequently resemble a marriage that ends in a messy divorce. After practicing law 15 years before becoming a professor, this author suggests, based on experience, that joint ventures are generally to be avoided. In the next few chapters we shall take a look at international sales transactions that are the legal basis for exporting and the legal basics of international investments. Finally, the last chapter shall be a brief look at the emerging area of electronic commerce.

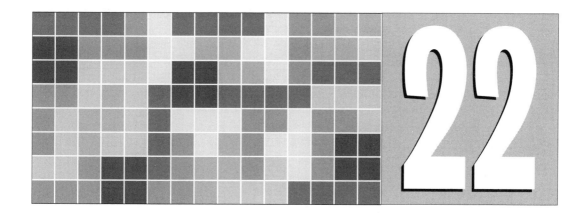

A Guidebook to International Sales Transactions

The heart of modern international trade is the legal and financial structure for the sales transaction. The entire transaction, including the sales contract, financing, and transportation can be similar to a domestic transaction, but it is complicated by the influence of any number of legal factors encountered along the journey. For example, the legal system of the seller's country may enter into the transaction in addition to the legal system of other nations controlling the financing organizations, insurance providers, shipping companies, freight forwarders and customs procedures.

UNCISG

As under most legal systems, the international sales transaction begins with a contract. The international sales contract need not be complicated. Unless the parties state otherwise, and they often should state otherwise, the

United Nations Convention for the International Sale of Goods (UNCISG) will govern the contract.

As is generally true of most of the world's legal systems, a contract under the UNCISG begins with an offer and an acceptance. The offer need not be complete in all its terms. The UNCISG requires only that an offer describe the goods, fix quantity and a price, and indicate in some way that a contract will be formed if the offer is accepted. If the parties fail to specify other contract requirements, such as the terms of delivery, or who pays for shipping, the UNCISG has provisions that determine such issues even when the contract makes no mention of them.

A few other provisions of the UNCISG require attention. Disturbingly, it has no requirement for any type of sales contract to be in writing. A number of countries, but not the United States, have adopted the treaty with reservations so that their courts are not necessarily bound by oral contracts. Also, the seller is obligated to provide insurance for the goods while they are being transported in the performance of a contract subject to the UNCISG unless the seller discloses that it is not providing such insurance. In that case the seller must give the buyer any necessary information needed for the buyer to purchase insurance. If the contract is silent about the time for delivery, the UNCISG presumes a "reasonable" time.

When goods arrive the buyer is, under the terms of the UNCISG, afforded a reasonable time to inspect the goods and may refuse delivery if they do not materially conform to the terms of the contract. If the contract does not specify a price, the court may still enforce the contract by assigning a sales price based on previous sales of similar goods in the same market. If the contract is silent as to the time of payment it is presumed to be simultaneous with delivery. If the contract is silent about when risk of loss passes to the buyer, the UNCISG usually presumes risk to pass at the point when the seller has delivered the goods to the first carrier if transportation of the goods is necessary to perform the contract. If transport is not necessary the risk passes in accordance with the INCO term, EXW, as described in the following list.

The UNCISG normally applies only to the commercial sale of most types of goods. It specifically does not apply to household goods, sales by auction, contracts for the sale of real estate or labor, ships, aircraft, or electricity.

In the author's opinion the UNCISG is seriously flawed as contract law because it applies a cultural test to determine the meaning of the contract. In other words, the contract means what it means to a person of the type that it is to be enforced against rather than the plain meaning of the words. This pliable interpretation could easily lead to lawsuits based on claims of the subtleties of cultural differences. In order to avoid such a result, the parties to any international sale should seriously consider specifying another, mutually agreeable, body of law to control contract disputes. The UNCISG allows the parties to expressly choose any mutually agreeable body of law to control their contract, such as the Uniform Commercial Code as adopted by the state of New York, United States, to control disputes arising from the contract.

INCO TERMS

The avoidance of conflicts in international sales transactions requires that the contract delineate exactly who is to pay for what aspect of the transportation process.

Promulgated by the International Chamber of Commerce (which accounts for the name), INCO terms have been translated into all major languages used for global commerce. The parties to a contract, can, by including a simple three-letter abbreviation in their contract, precisely define many of their responsibilities in a way that most any court can read in its native language. The terms are simple and can be easily understood and applied.

Here is a brief description of each INCO term beginning with the one that imposes the greatest obligations on the buyer and ending with those that impose the greatest obligations on the seller.

- **EXW** (Ex Works): When goods are sold EXW, the seller makes the good available to the buyer at the seller's place of business. The seller does not provide any transport or additional services, except the seller gives the buyer any documentation that the buyer needs to clear customs.

- **FCA** (Free Carrier): The seller provides transport at seller's expense only to the carrier named in the contract. Risk of loss passes to the buyer when the carrier takes possession of the goods.

- **FAS** (Free Alongside Ship): The seller is obligated to transport the goods at seller's expense and risk to the dock or quay where the ship that will further transport the goods is, or will be, berthed. Upon arrival at the quay all responsibility for expense and loss passes to the buyer.

- **FOB** (Free on Board): Applicable only to water transportation, and usually naming the port of departure, the seller's obligations end when the seller arranges for loading at seller's expense, and the goods have passed over the ship's rail. The buyer pays for all further expenses to transport the goods to the destination and assumes risk of loss when the goods pass the ship's rail upon being loaded. If the goods are not hoisted over the ship's rail, such as in roll-on/roll-off operations, FCA is a more appropriate term.

- **CFR** (Cost and Freight): Usually naming a place of arrival when goods are shipped CFR, the seller must pay the expenses of shipping the goods to the named destination but risk of loss passes when the goods pass the ship's rail, just as if the goods were shipped FOB.

- **CIF** (Cost, Insurance, and Freight): Usually naming a place of arrival, CIF imposes nearly the same obligations as CFR. The difference is that under CIF the seller becomes obligated to provide an insurance policy to protect the buyer from risk of loss while the goods are in transit. CIF applies to water transport; the land transport equivalent is CIP (Carriage and Insurance Paid To).

- **DAF** (Delivered at Frontier): DAF obligates the seller to deliver the goods to a precisely named point near the border, prior to the payment of customs duties. Risk of loss passes when the goods are safely delivered to the named point.

- **DES** (Delivered Ex Ship): The seller's obligations end under a DES contract if the goods are made available to the buyer on the ship that arrives at a named port. The seller pays the expenses necessary to get the goods to that point. The buyer is responsible for the risk and expenses involved in unloading the goods from the ship and completing the journey.

- **DEQ** (Delivered Ex Quay): A sale DEQ is similar to DES but includes an obligation that the seller pays for unloading and, if and only if specified in the contract, clearing customs and paying any duty. Risk of loss passes when the goods are unloaded from the ship at the named port of destination.

- **DDU** (Deliver Duty Unpaid): Combined with a named place, the seller's obligations and risk end when the goods are delivered to that named place. The seller has no obligation to clear customs for the buyer, but the parties should take great care to choose the named place of delivery. They should make certain that it is a place where the goods can be legally delivered without first clearing customs. If a DDU contract names a delivery point where customs must be cleared to enter, the contract is inherently ambiguous.

- **DDP** (Deliver Duty Paid): DDP, with a named destination, requires the most from the seller of any INCO term. A DDP contract requires the seller to make all transportation arrangements, and get the goods through customs with duty paid. The seller pays all expenses associated with the movement of the goods. Risk of loss remains with the seller until the goods are offered for delivery at the destination named in the contract. The seller should not agree to sell DDP without being completely familiar with the expenses and procedures of making delivery to the named destination.

THE LETTER OF CREDIT TRANSACTION

The perpetual problem to be solved in any international sales transaction is how to provide security to both the buyer and seller that each will perform their part of the transaction if the other one already has. The buyer is concerned that if payment is sent first, the seller will not ship the goods. The seller is concerned that if the goods are shipped before payment is received the buyer will not pay. The best solution to this problem has been the use of a letter of credit under the rules of the International Chamber of Commerce (ICC).

The ICC has been promulgating rules in this area since 1933 with the latest incarnation of its scheme of rules, the fifth, called Uniform Customs and Practices for Documentary Credits (UCP). The entire text of the rules for the use of letters of credit may be obtained from the ICC. Use of letters of credit is a complex legal topic but for purposes of this overview, the following description of the process is sufficient.

Again, the purpose of a letter of credit transaction is to assure both the buyer and the seller that the other will perform the obligations under the sales contract. The seller becomes assured that the buyer will pay if the seller ships when a letter of credit is issued. The issuance of a letter of credit means that a bank guarantees payment to the seller when the contract is fulfilled; thereby negating any need to trust the buyer. The buyer is assured that the product will be shipped if payment is made, because the bank will not release funds to the seller until the seller furnishes documentation proving that the goods have been shipped, usually in the form of a bill of lading from a carrier.

THE LETTER OF CREDIT PROCESS

The buyer is always the one who obtains the letter of credit because a letter of credit is used to make payment. The buyer initiates the process by asking the bank to issue a letter of credit in favor of the seller. The letter of credit will list certain conditions, normally the presentation of the documents, which the seller must meet in order for the bank to make payment. The bank agrees, however, that when the seller meets the conditions of the letter of credit it will make payment regardless of the disposition of the buyer. Often, the issuing bank may ask a bank in the seller's country to make the seller aware of the existence of the letter of credit. The bank giving such notice to the seller is called an advisory bank.

A letter of credit obligates a bank to make payment on behalf of the buyer, therefore the bank will expect the buyer to ultimately reimburse it for funds dispersed on the buyer's behalf. Naturally, the bank will not issue a letter of credit without some assurance that the buyer is creditworthy. This assurance could be in the form of a cash deposit, collateral, or a satisfactory record of payment for past transactions.

To obtain payment, the seller delivers the goods consistent with the terms of the letter of credit and obtains the documents specified in the letter of credit, which are then presented to the issuing bank or its representative bank. Normally among the list of documents is a bill of lading issued by a carrier, which indicates that the carrier has received the goods and has begun the process of shipment to the buyer. The bill of lading lists the buyer or its bank as the consignee who is entitled to delivery when the goods arrive. The letter of credit may list and require presentation of any number of other documents needed by the buyer to clear customs, assure quality and so on.

A banker at either the issuing or advisory bank then checks the documents to ensure that they conform to the requirements of the letter of credit. If all is in order, payment is authorized for the seller and reimbursement for the bank is required of the buyer. When the buyer has satisfied the bank that payment will be made to the bank, the buyer is given the bill of lading, which the bank obtained from the seller. The buyer will present this document to obtain delivery.

In conformance with the "Tour" theme of this book, a simplified description of the process of international sales transactions is provided. Many excellent books treat this subject in detail. A good place to begin is with publication UCP 500 from the International Chamber of Commerce. A more detailed description of the mechanics of the letter of credit process may be read in this author's book, A *Tour of International Trade.*

A Guidebook to International Investment

In some parts of the world foreign private investments are among the more controversial business activities. In recent years almost no other business activities have undergone such major changes in their regulatory scheme as have foreign private investment in much of the developing world. Many of these changes in regulations were in response to changes in political and economic philosophy.

Following the Second World War, Japan embarked on a strategy of reconstruction wherein it established a high level of tariff protection and severe restrictions on foreign investments. The idea was to reserve the Japanese domestic market for struggling Japanese producers. The theoretical basis for this policy was that if these infant industries could be guaranteed to sell products in the domestic market they would gain economies of scale and expertise. Eventually they would develop to the point where they could compete successfully in the world markets, and then Japan could become a major exporter. In Japan this policy seemed to work. Japan's post-war development was termed an *economic miracle*, and by the 1970s Japan's economy was among the most powerful in the world. Developing nations, which had generally few restrictions on foreign investment during the 1950s and 1960s, took note.

It seemed the secret for rapid economic progress had been revealed: less developed nations all over the world adopted the apparently successful policies of high tariffs and severe restrictions on foreign investment. Adding fuel to the process, many governments leaned to more socialist policies during the same period. Policies were often adopted reflecting a belief that private companies were merely profiteers designed to exploit the workers and resources of a developing nation while giving little in return.

Governments wanted to ensure that private business acted in the interests of the people of a host country. To that end, regulations were adopted requiring that foreign investments be reviewed and approved by an agency of the host government. Approval came only if, in the eyes of the government, the proposed new investments were not excessively disruptive to existing business and would fulfill a need in a way that was beneficial to the development of the country. If an investment was approved, the foreign investors were often required to find a local partner who would retain a controlling interest in the company to further limit the exploitive powers of the foreigners. These local partners frequently could or would not advance much money toward launching the enterprise.

Many important industries in developing nations were nationalized, often without compensation to the owners. After nationalization the industries were often granted monopoly status and managed directly by the government, presumably so that the best interests of the country and its people could be the only consideration in management decisions.

Such policies unleashed a host of unintended consequences. Often the criterion used in selection and approval of foreign investment proposals seemed all too rarely to meet the needs of the host country. Frequently, government approval was dependent on the number and size of various bribes, and the number of friends and relatives of powerful people chosen as the local partners. The economic basis of the investment was often barely a factor in the process.

Government management of state-owned industries was usually incompetent at best and completely corrupt as worst. Often operating at huge losses, state-owned industries drained away government resources sorely needed for other purposes while their monopoly and subsidized status kept more efficient producers from entering their reserved markets.

At first glance one would think that a company could circumvent restrictions on importing or direct investment by licensing a domestic producer to produce one's products locally and profit through collection of licensing fees. Unfortunately, most developing countries also had weak intellectual property protection. All too often the result of licensing was merely to train the domestic licensee to become a competitor after it learned the business.

Rather than protect the people, investment regulatory laws often had the consequence of creating a difficult, dangerous, and hostile environment for foreign participation in business within the country. By the 1980s the flow of foreign investment into developing nations fell far below what was needed for either development or improvement in domestic employment problems. Making matters worse, the domestic producers did not flourish in most countries as they had in Japan.

Weak intellectual property protection meant that many patent holders refused to introduce their new technology in countries where they feared it might be stolen. The developing nations fell further and further behind the world in the use of new technology. The developing country's domestic producers, freed by tariff and investment law from foreign competition, often produced shoddy products that they sold for relatively high prices. These producers had no economic incentive to improve the quality and technology of their products and no incentive to reduce their prices. Domestic consumers had no possibility to substitute imports for the poor bargains exclusively offered them and their standard of living suffered. Needless to say, the domestic producers usually did not improve to the point where they could export, which was the objective of the scheme to protect domestic industries.

The 1980s saw a series of economic and political crises take place in the developing world. These circumstances precipitated change. Rule by rule, nations dropped restrictions on the type of enterprises in which foreigners were allowed to invest. Requirements for government approval were eased or dropped. One hundred percent foreign ownership was again allowed. Many state-owned industries were stripped of their monopoly status and sold to private investors, often to foreign interests.

In the developed world, restrictions on foreign investment have usually remained much less onerous, although many nations, including the United States, have some restrictions on foreign investment. Such restrictions often center on industries developing or marketing military technology, or on other national security issues. The trend worldwide, however, is to reduce barriers to foreign investment as a means of attracting economic activity, particularly employers, to one's country.

Unlike international sales, which have an extensive body of international law governing them and the World Trade Organization enforcing the rules, little true international law regulates foreign investment. A precedent establishes an obligation for a nation to take reasonable measures to protect foreign investors, and foreign investments within its borders, from violence, at least to the extent it protects its own citizens. Beyond that, a number of nations have entered into bilateral investment treaties with other nations to set mutual standards for the protection of each other's investors in the contracting nations. These treaties often give national treatment to investors from other contracting nations and have preference over other national laws. Although containing no outright prohibitions to the nationalization of private investments, many bilateral investment treaties provide for prompt, adequate, and effective compensation in the event of government confiscation of an investment owned by an investor from another contracting party.

Trade blocs frequently include protection for investors in the treaties that form the legal basis for the organization. Advanced agreements to regionalize economies, such as the European Union, NAFTA, and MERCOSUR, often guarantee access to business in the other parties' territory by investors of any member. Such agreements also provide extensive protections for the rights of investors and a mechanism for settlement of disputes that arise between investors and their host governments.

Finally investors should consider a host nation's fear of adverse publicity in today's investment climate. Today, many nations compete to provide a fertile place for investment. In order to be hospitable to investors, national law now often supplements international in law protecting foreign investments. All law protecting foreign investment is rapidly developing as an instrument for governments to assure investors that their country is a good place to bring new money and jobs. A nation's fear of losing it reputation as a good place for business to locate might prove to be as protective as the words in a law book.

A Guidebook to International Enforcement of Intellectual Property Rights

No matter what motivated you to to buy this text, the author, editors, proof-readers, printers, marketing people, and many others spent countless hours on the production of this book. Most of those whose hard work brought you this book support themselves by helping to produce books and, quite un-derstandably, want to be paid for the work. Without the issuance of a few paychecks, it is unlikely that you would find this book, or many others, on your favorite bookstore's shelves, or something new to watch at the movies, or an interesting and novel new gadget to connect to your computer.

The law promotes the concept that those who conceive or distribute valuable creative thoughts should be rewarded for the effort expended. The reward comes in the form of being designated as the only ones permitted to sell the exact form of their creative thoughts for a period of time. This chapter explores the application of that concept in the international arena.

It is a relatively recent and western concept that one could actually have commercial ownership of one's creative thoughts. Based on the practical idea that people would be more creative if they were better paid to create, the first patent law came into existence in England in 1623 and is known as the Statute of Monopolies. Nearly 100 years later, in 1710, the first copyright law surfaced in the form of Statute of Anne. Early intellectual property laws were quite limited. Over the subsequent years the variety of intellectual property that may be protected has grown substantially. The amount of protection increased as well, at least in most of the Western world. Since the eighteenth century, dramatic growth in the amount of protection available in the United States has occurred. For example, the original United States Copyright Act of 1790 established protection for only 14 years though it could be renewed for an additional 14-year term if the author was still living. Now, under some circumstances, a United States copyright is good for the life of the author plus 70 additional years.

In today's world, intellectual property rights are classified into four categories as follows:

1. *Patents* give an inventor an exclusive right to use the invention for a fixed period of time. In exchange, the inventor must make public the details of the invention. After the expiration of the fixed period of time, which is 20 years for members of World Trade Organization, the entire world is free to use the invention in any way they wish.

2. *Trademarks and service marks* are intended to distinguish the source of goods and services so they are not confused with others. They can be words such as brand names, symbols such as logos, or even a sound such as a bit of music or a distinctive product design that adds style but not any new function.

3. *Copyrights* are an exclusive right to reproduce an original creative work in a tangible medium of expression such as music, literature, or art. The ideas are not protected by a copyright, only the way in which they are described. Members of the World Trade Organization receive copyright protection for at least the author's life plus 50 years if the copyright is owned by a person. Companies may hold a copyright for 50 years.

4. *Trade secrets* are information not generally known and kept secret, such as the exact recipe for a brand of soft drink. Trade secrets receive vary-

ing levels of protection in different countries depending upon the efforts the owner has made to keep the information secret and the means used by others to learn it. Due to the varying nature of trade secret protection it is not possible to describe the world's law concerning trade secrets in a general way in this book.

The enforcement mechanism for intellectual property rights has, until quite recently, been a hodgepodge of national laws and regional or bilateral treaties. Generally, rights have been better enforced in the Western world than in the East, where individual ownership of creative expression is somewhat alien to the prevailing collective and Confucian philosophy.

A complex system protects rights to use one's creative thoughts commercially in today's world. We shall explore the system, beginning with patents.

PATENTS

Patents are issued to protect inventors of new design or technology who have produced a new product or process. Once recognized by a national government or regional authority, a patent gives the inventor the exclusive right to make, use, distribute, or sell products based on the technology protected by the patent within the nation or region. Patents are issued only if the technology is genuinely new and useful. The requirement of newness simply means that the technology is outside the body of existing knowledge, in other words not part of the prior state of the art.

In most countries, national governments or regional institutions first grant patents. In much of Europe, applications are made through the European Patent Office. In parts of Africa patents are applied for through the African Regional Industrial Property Organization. In most other regions applications are made through a patent office operated by the national government.

Similarities can be found in the process of obtaining of a patent regardless of jurisdiction. The only differences are in the details. The first step is usually the filing of a patent application. The application usually contains a title for the invention, a designation of its technical field, background information regarding the state of the art, a description of the invention, various drawings or other visual illustrations, and a statement of what the inventor claims to have invented. A review of any existing technology follows. If the process confirms the inventor's claims that the invention is truly a new idea a patent is issued. The patent protects the technology for some period of time, usually 20 years.

A difference between the United States and much of the rest of the world regards who is entitled to a patent for new technology. In much of the world the first person to file an application is usually granted the patent. In the United States the patent is issued to the first person who actually did the inventing regardless of who filed the first application. The procedure used in the United States leads to disputes about who invented first, but it provides a remedy if the technology is stolen and the thief makes the first application. The dispute between the United States and much of the rest of the world over this procedure presents a major problem in attempts to harmonize patent procedures with the goal of providing worldwide protection.

In much of Europe, patents are registered according to the European Patent Convention (ECP). The ECP's present members include Austria, Belgium, Switzerland, Cyprus, Germany, Denmark, Spain, Finland, France, Turkey, Greece, Ireland, Italy, Liechtenstein, Luxembourg, Monaco, Netherlands, Portugal, Sweden, and United Kingdom. In the process of joining EPC are Albania, Lithuania, Latvia, Macedonia, Romania, and Slovenia.

A patent application filed with the EPC provides protection in any member country requested by the requested applicant in its application.

The African Regional Intellectual Property Agreement provides protection in Botswana, Gambia, Ghana, Kenya, Lesotho, Malawi, Sierra Leone, Somalia, Sudan, Swaziland, Uganda, United Republic of Tanzania, Zambia, and Zimbabwe.

Wider protection of patent rights can be obtained through the Paris Convention, adopted by more than 100 countries. Members of the Paris Convention agree to give national treatment to foreigners from other participating countries. (For a discussion of "national treatment" see the introduction to Section V.) Also, the date on which an inventor originally applied for the patent in the inventor's home member country becomes the application date used for subsequent applications in all "first to file" countries as long as subsequent applications are made within 12 months of that first application date. Under the Paris Convention, the inventor must still file applications individually in each country where protection is desired. As stated before, however, the inventor may use the date of first application in the home country for 12 months for "first to file" purposes.

Another route to wider patent protection is a filing through the Patent Cooperation Treaty (PCT) administered by the World Intellectual Property Organization (WIPO). WIPO is an agency of the United Nations and is headquartered in Geneva, Switzerland. The PCT has been in effect since 1978. This agreement presently has more than 90 member nations. The PCT centralizes the filing of multiple patent applications in a number of official receiving offices. It has also standardized the application format, making it much easier for patent protection to be obtained in a multitude of places with a standard filing in just one place.

Another route to wider patent protection is through the new Agreement on Trade-Related Aspects of Intellectual Property Rights (TRIPS), which was engendered by the Uruguay round of negotiations that also resulted in the creation of the World Trade Organization. TRIPS require WTO members to respect the Paris Convention and to grant at least 20 years of protection to new technology and 10 years to new industrial designs.

National governments are required by TRIPS to make their intellectual property laws enforceable, and penalties for infringement must be tough enough to deter future violations. Violations of intellectual property rights on a commercial scale must be a criminal offense and a nation's courts must have the right to destroy counterfeit goods. TRIPS also permits aggrieved members to enforce their rights through the World Trade Organization's dispute resolution mechanism.

Trademarks

Trademarks are words, brand names, symbols, sounds, or colors that identify the origin of goods or services. Once they have been established, trademarks, unlike patents, have a perpetual life so long as they are continuously used in business.

The first step in the protection of one's trademarks is to choose a trademark that is legally capable of protection. Some nation's laws are more liberal than others are when it comes to the type of trademark that can be protected. Most nations would protect the symbol of the Golden Arches of McDonald's restaurant, but many would be quite reluctant to grant the exclusive use of the name McDonald's to a foreign corporation. Doing so could deny one of their citizens, who is named McDonald, the right to operate a restaurant using that name.

Another problem arises when a trademark includes the name of a geographic place. Many nations prohibit, through their criminal law, any mention of a geographic place in the name of a product unless that place is the actual physical origin of the trademarked product. Even if such a practice is permitted, many courts are reluctant to allow a private party to exclusively use the name of a place where many people live. For example, a name like "Texas Barbeque Company" could not be used as a trademark in many places unless the meat was actually produced in Texas. And if another company advertised Texas barbeque many courts would be reluctant to say that one party has the exclusive right to the name "Texas."

An interesting series of litigation on this issue has continued in various forms for more than 100 years over the right to use the name of the Czechoslovakian town of Budvar. In German, one who comes from Budvar is a *Budweiser*, a trade name used simultaneously by the American company Anheuser-Busch and a Czech company Budejovicky Budvar. Anheuser-Busch began using the name in 1876 in America, and the Czech company Gudejovidcky Budvar started brewing a Budweiser beer in Europe in 1895. Because Budejovicky Budvar actually produces the beer in Budvar it claims that Anheuser-Busch has violated European origin rules and has won the right to use the name in most of Europe. The law in the Americas and Asia generally favors Anheuser-Busch, since it was the first to use the name. The litigation continues.

Another frequent source of trouble is the choice of a trademark that sounds like a mere a description of the goods. The exclusive use of a name like "Tasty Burgers" might be successfully challenged by a competitor who claims that the designation of the competitor's product as a "tasty burger" in advertising is merely a description of the product and not an infringement of the other trademark.

To be safe, we could use a trademark that means nothing outside the context of our product such as "Xerox" or "Exxon." Still, our marketing department would probably prefer a trademark that raises some positive image in the customer's mind. As a compromise between legal protection and marketing savvy consider for example the movie studio's trade name "Dreamworks." If we avoid the pitfalls of common surnames, geographical places, or descriptive names we can probably establish a trademark that will protected in much of the world.

Historically a trademark had to be registered in each country where it was used and protection was afforded only in countries where it was registered. Efforts to globalize the registration and protection of trademarks began in the nineteenth century with the Paris Convention in 1883. The Paris Convention requires its members to give national treatment to foreigners seeking trademark protection within their borders. A number of provisions in the Paris Convention are important in this regard, most notably Articles 6 and 10.

Article 6 provides that the owner of a "well known" trademark must be protected from a later user of the mark even if the mark was not registered. This article establishes a basis for protection even if the mark was not previously registered in the country. This provision benefits owners of world-famous brands whose products are being faked by a local counterfeiter in a country where they have not yet marketed the product. Article 10 of the Paris Convention is a blanket prohibition against "unfair competition" in the use of trademarks. This provision seems to mean whatever the judge in any particular country and case thinks it means. Even though not legally precise, Article 10 may create a legal cause of action for one whose products are being counterfeited when no clear remedy exists in local law.

Many U. S. companies are ignorant of the Madrid Agreement for the International Registration of Trademark Rights (MAIRTA), because the United States is not a member, but MAIRTA is an important treaty in the area of trademark protection. MAIRTA members' citizens can make a single trademark registration in their home countries and receive protection in all MAIRTA member countries. However, some aspects of MAIRTA conflict with U.S. trademark law, and the United States, as well as some other important trading nations, such as the United Kingdom and Japan, have refused to ratify MAIRTA.

The lack of participation by these important countries has inspired a new version of the Madrid Agreement, popularly known as the Madrid Protocol, which cures or lessens many of the objections potential members have to joining MAIRTA. The United States finds the Madrid Protocol much more palatable than MAIRTA, and legislation is presently pending in the U.S. Congress to accept and ratify the Madrid Protocol. If adopted, the Madrid Protocol would allow U. S. businesses to file for protection in the other member countries with their application for protection in the United States and eliminate the expense and filing fees associated with multiple filings as is presently required.

Protection of trademarks in the European Union is obtainable either country by country, or with a single filing of a Community Trademark of the European Union (CTM). A CTM may be filed in any EU member country's trademark registration office. It may be filed by one who is, or is not, a citizen of the European Union. Trademarks that are deemed to be descriptive will not be accepted for registration as a CTM. CTMs that conflict with existing trademarks in one of the member states will be denied as well, but in that case the application may be converted into an application for a national trademark in the country of filing. Once registered, a CTM provides protection throughout the EU. The European Union is a member of the Paris Convention, the Madrid Agreement, and the Madrid Protocol, thus a registration of a CTM may give the registrant access to protection by all four international agreements.

COPYRIGHTS

Copyrights protect authors, composers, and artists who have tangibly expressed their creative works by writing, sculpting, painting, or otherwise preserving them in some solid, durable form. Facts and information cannot be copyrighted. Only the way the facts and information are expressed is subject to copyright. It is perfectly legal to express information found elsewhere with your own organization and words.

Once created, copyrights may be bought and sold or licensed to another for payments called royalties. Copyrights have a certain lifespan under the law. This lifespan varies from country to country, but according to the World Intellectual Property Organization guidelines, copyrights should generally last at least for 50 years after the death of the author. Some national laws establish longer time limits, although shorter limits exist in many nations for specific types of copyrights such as the rights to television broadcasts.

A directive of the European Union requires all member states to recognize copyrights for 70 years from the death of the author except for sound recordings and broadcasts. These latter categories of intellectual property are protected for 50 years from publication in the case of recordings, or 50 years from the end of the year in which the broadcast took place.

The owner of a copyright can prohibit or permit the reproduction, public performance, recording, broadcasting, or translation of a copyrighted work.

No legal formality is required to protect one's copyright. Creative works are legally protected from the moment they are created. As a practical matter, it is often wise to register a work with a governmental authority to better establish the fact that one was the first to create it. In the United States, such registration is done through the Copyright Office of the Library of Congress and other nations have similar registration authorities.

Because many individual authors and artists do not have the means to register and protect their copyrights, a number of collective management organizations have been set up, usually specializing in one type of intellectual property, to help their members register and protect their rights.

The international protection of copyrights is done through the auspices of the Berne Convention, which first emerged in 1886, and through the previously mentioned Agreement on Trade-Related Aspects of International Property Rights (TRIPS).

The Berne Convention for the Protection of Literary and Artistic Works is known throughout the world as simply the Berne Convention. It has, as its basis, three basic principles:

1. Each member nation must give protection to works that originate in other member nations. This protection must be the same treatment the nation gives works originating within its own borders. In other words, works must receive national treatment.

2. No member nation may require any formal procedure before works from other member nations are protected.

3. Foreign works must be protected according to local law even if they are not protected in their home country. However, if the work is protected in the home country the time period of protection under the law of the home country may be applied if it is less than the protection granted in the foreign country.

The Berne Convention also sets out the minimum standards of protection that a member nation may afford works from other member nations as follows:

> The protection must include every production in the literary, scientific and artistic domain whatever may be the mode or form of its expression.

The following rights are reserved to the copyright holder:

- The right to translate
- The right to make adaptations or changes to the work
- The right to perform in public, dramatico-musical and musical works

- The right to recite in public literary works

- The right to communicate to the public the performance of such works

- The right to broadcast

- The right to reproduce

- The right to use the work as the basis for audiovisual work

- "Moral rights" such as the right to claim authorship

Developing countries are excused from prohibitions against translating and reproduction under some conditions.

The TRIPS agreement has imposed additional conditions on nations that are members of the World Trade Organization. WTO members must extend most favored nation status to other WTO members. This has the effect of extending any protection granted by any WTO member to any other WTO member to all WTO members. TRIPS effectively makes any bilateral or regional treaty into a worldwide obligation for WTO members.

TRIPS has special provisions requiring protection of computer programs and motion pictures.

Finally, under the TRIPS agreement any intellectual property, except art and photographs, must be protected for at least 50 years from the date of first publication or date of creation.

Enforcement of intellectual property rights has not been uniform throughout the world. Some nations strictly enforce them, while other nations have been notably lax. The tendency in recent years has been for an increasing number of nations to join intellectual property agreements, partly because doing so is often made a condition for joining such organizations as the World Trade Organization. Even in China, where an old folk saying says, "The theft of a book is an elegant crime," joined the Berne Convention in 1992. Even though this action may have been only part of an effort to bolster its application to the WTO rather than a change in philosophy, China's accession does signal a change in how eastern governments are thinking. New challenges to the intellectual property enforcement scheme have been posed in recent years by the proliferation in computer and other technology. One might expect many changes in the law and treaties to cope with such changes.

Index

NetEffect is the training solution that can help your organization distinguish itself from your competition.

- An extensive library of training and reference materials designed around your needs
- Satisfies your need for brighter, more informed, and better trained employees
- Ideal for corporate environments, NetEffect can be used for self-study or in teams